Ad

for

Your True Self Is Enough

This is a beautifully written and deeply personal memoir. It is also a guidebook for families in the throes of adjusting to the diagnosis, early intervention, and challenges of their young child, while navigating all new systems and providers. Easy to read and full of so much to learn about resources, relationships, and resilience. It's been said that there's no instruction manual for raising children—especially unique and neurodivergent ones. This book is a significant and important contribution to the empowerment of parents of these children.

–Ellen K. Reinstein, LCSW
Former Director, Current Clinical Consultant &
Supervisor, Cheerful Helpers Child & Family Center

Warm, honest, and compassionate, Your True Self Is Enough *is an amazing book that needs to be out there for all the other parents on this journey! Captivating and engaging, it's like listening to a friend share her story over coffee. The way this story unfolds, with brief 'truth corners' throughout, allows the reader to receive helpful tips without judgment or pressure—truly unique in the space of 'parenting books' that often leave struggling family members feeling more stressed with long to-do lists and regrets. Lovell shares many real-life, big, heavy, scary challenges in this book that other families may also face, and still leaves the reader feeling optimistic and grateful!*

–Kimberli Breen, MS, CAS, MA
School Psychologist and National Behavior Change Agent

This book is glorious! Raw and authentic. Lovell's willingness to admit those thoughts and fears that we all feel but are ashamed to admit openly and publicly provided me with such a release, while her "Truth Bombs" provide guidance, love, support and tools to help find a way to make the world adjust to us instead of the other way around. Your True Self Is Enough *is an important piece of writing that will be so helpful for so many people struggling as parents of special children—because ALL of our children are special. Parents of neurotypical children will get as much out of this as any other parent.*

–Brian Altounian
Podcast Host, "Just Two Dads"

A beautiful memoir—a love letter.

–Jackie Sloan
Founder/Director
www.thechildrensranch.org

Here I am with tears after being glued to Lovell's words from page one. What a beautiful love letter—raw, relatable, and inspiring. These words will resonate with so many people.

–Shetal Parikh, MSW
Special Education Teacher

Susanna writes beautifully and honestly about her dreams for motherhood, the unexpected realities and how she comes to love herself and her daughter. A powerful book, with practical advice for all parents, and especially those facing unplanned challenges.

–Janet Upjohn, LCSW
Executive Director, Cheerful Helpers
Child and Family Study Center

Forward

My daughter A. had some advice she wanted to share with readers of this book. Here are a few of her thoughts.

- No child is perfect and no human is perfect. It's OK to not be perfect, but you should always be respectful.

- If someone's brain works a little differently, and they behave a little differently, that doesn't mean they're not a good person. They just might not really understand.

- Your true self is enough. You shouldn't have to change yourself to make other people happy.

- Learn to understand your child rather than make them do what you think is normal.

- Listen.

- Ableism is when people are being mean to others because of their abilities and it's not nice. I feel like we should just accept people regardless of who they are. Any type of discrimination needs to go away.

- There's a place for you in this world and don't give up. You don't need to be ashamed of being different—everybody is.

- Don't underestimate people because they are different. Because you are also different. Everybody's different. Nobody's the same.

Introduction

I was always obsessed with Christmas.

Every year, I would toss aside my sister's sheet music and grab her wiry silver violin stand. Then I'd drape the crocheted green blanket that brought me home from St. John's Hospital as a baby over the stand's top, letting the pointy parts match up with the holes in the blanket's design. Next came the neon whistle-necklace I had earned playing endless rounds of Skee-Ball at Chuck E. Cheese. There was the red yo-yo, a lovely hanging piece, that I wrapped around my tree twice. Snoopy, my small but oh-so-cherished squishy stuffed animal, had a red tinsel string attached to his head: the ideal detail for hanging him to my tree. I would finish my spindly, sparkly violin stand with ribbons and fabric I'd hoarded from my mother's stash in our hallway closet.

"Perfect," I'd think to myself.

In the church I grew up in, we didn't celebrate most holidays because they weren't considered to be literal translations from the bible. Christmas, in fact, was considered to be the most secular and worldly holiday of them all.

Though we weren't allowed to watch much television and weren't exposed to much media in general back then, I had learned about Christmas at the mall. Every year, South Coast Plaza transformed into a Winter Wonderland. Reindeer replaced the carousel horses and Santa was sitting in his workshop where elves handed out candy canes. Gift boxes, some almost as big as me, were everywhere.

My whole life I had pined for Christmas. And then, one Sunday in May when I was nine years old, Christmas showed up at my house.

The doorbell rang unexpectedly on that early spring evening. My siblings and I were finishing up our dinner chores and my parents were getting organized for the week ahead. I liked to think of myself as the mayor of the house, so I rushed to the door and flung it wide open.

There stood a stranger in a suit holding a basket so huge I could only see the top of his head.

"Is Mrs. Sandra Yang here?" said a voice from behind the basket.

I didn't respond because I was in awe. I'd never seen anything quite like this basket in my life. There were chocolates, nuts, wine, and candy. There were lotions, soaps, and bath salts. There were heaps of meticulously gift-wrapped packages in a rainbow of colors, glitter, and silky bows. It was… *Christmas.*

"Is your mother home?" the man asked again.

I snapped back to reality and called out to my mom. She came in from the kitchen, slowly drying her hands on her apron, and furrowed her brow.

"Yes?" she asked. "Can I help you?"

"Mrs. Yang, congratulations! Your daughter Susanna won the Macy's Mother's Day Contest, and we are here to present you with the grand-prize-winning basket!"

I'd already forgotten about how, a few months prior, my third-grade class had participated in a Mother's Day contest. The rules were simple: draw a picture and describe a scenario that answers the question, "What makes your mother the best in the world?"

I spent hours drawing myself as a glamorous girl in a low-waisted dress with a polka-dot bubble skirt and pink and purple bows in my hair. I drew my mom lovingly stroking my back. Below the picture, I wrote: *My mommy is the best mother in the world because she always comforts me and makes me feel safe and loved. She rubs my back and says "there there" to make me feel better especially when I'm feeling sad or sick. She is always there for me.*

I had always dreamed about having kids of my own. I knew I would be good at it. And I was already such a "little mommy" to my four siblings. I changed diapers, babysat, shushed, comforted and played imaginary games with my three sisters and brother. It never felt like work and I had endless energy and patience.

And on that day I won the Macy's prize, I learned that being a good mother was rewarded! I didn't think it was extraordinary, what my mother was to me. She always made me feel taken care of. But apparently it *was* special because now I had won this basket full of Christmas for my mother. One day I was going to be a spectacular mother too and *everyone* would know it.

Chapter 1

I N THE '90s, there was a lot of talk about what would
happen when the year 2000 came around. Would the
world fall apart? Would computer systems around the
country crash and burn? But all I could think about was the fact
that in the year 2000, I would be 26 years old. "Wow," I would
think. "That must mean I will be a mother already." Whenever
I imagined my life as an adult, I saw myself as a mother.

Whenever I was asked what I wanted to be when I grew
up, if I wasn't quickly answering "a mom!" with great convic-
tion, I was uttering the following two options: a police officer
"so I could yell at people and tell them what to do," or a bus
driver "so I could drive people around town and pull a cool
lever that would make the door open." When I grew older, I
also threw in the more appropriate and acceptable response:
"A pediatrician." If there isn't a better definition of mother
than police officer combined with bus driver and a sprinkling
of pediatric medicine, I don't know what it is.

But truthfully, this was my dream. Motherhood sounded
like such bliss to me. I never wavered from this desire and

would only consider my adulthood successful if I accomplished this dream.

As it turned out, Y2K came and went with little fanfare. In 2000, I was still far from being a mom: I was single and trying to figure out my path in life. I'd reached a level of financial security at an early age, rising up the ranks as a software sales consultant in burgeoning Silicon Valley shortly after I graduated from UC Berkeley. I'd just bought my first condo, on Lake Merritt in Oakland. I had lots of friends and a full life, but still I felt a void. When an opportunity came to move to Los Angeles, I took it as a sign that things were about to change for me.

And I was right. Only a few years later—and just a few months into newly-married bliss with my husband Brian—I was pregnant. I was ebullient...until I was introduced to morning sickness very soon thereafter.

I suddenly found my life scheduled around the act of puking. Pregnancy vomiting was so different from having the flu or a bad hangover. I felt grateful that my work place wasn't too far from my home because I couldn't bear to throw up at work. I didn't take lunch breaks anymore; instead I reserved 30-minute increments throughout the work day to drive home, throw up to my heart's content, brush my teeth, get back in my car and head back to the office. This was in addition to throwing up as soon as I woke up, after breakfast, before I left for work and multiple times after the work day was over. On good days, I only had to drive home once during work hours to purge. On bad days, I was making the round trip three times. I also had plastic bags on hand in case I couldn't make it to the bathroom. They were in my car, in every purse I carried, and throughout my home.

Eventually, I took a few weeks off to stay bedridden. Being idle was almost worse than being nauseated and busy. I had nothing else to do other than wallow in my miserable condition and wonder what was wrong with me.

My nine months of pregnancy weren't glamorous or blissed out the way I'd imagined they would be. Out of the 41 weeks of my pregnancy, I threw up for 36 of them. I gained so much weight on my small frame that I literally waddled everywhere. I found it so unfair that I had spent all this time with my head in the toilet and still managed to look and feel like a beached whale. My feet were swollen with retained water. I felt sick, anxious, and exhausted, and I cried all the time. I wanted the baby out of my body, just so I could have regular hormones again.

I called my mom multiple times a day. "Mom, I'm so ready for this baby to come!" I would whine to her.

"Ha," she would respond, and I imagined her mouth turning into a smile on the other end of the line. "Susanna. Enjoy this time before the baby comes. Trust me."

My girlfriend, Taedra, who had a one-year-old when I first shared my pregnancy news with her, tried to give me a similar warning. "Susanna," she said one day, "I had no idea what newborn life would be like, because nobody told me. I wish someone would have taken me by the shoulders, shaken me violently and screamed into my face, 'You have no idea that having a newborn is the hardest thing you will ever do in your entire life!' And then I wish they would have screamed the same thing to me every day until the baby was born, because I did not get it. I was so impatient for my baby to arrive."

I laughed when Taedra told me this. My mom and girlfriend didn't realize how ready I was for this life. I had mentally prepared myself to be a mother for 32 years. Even though I was experiencing a less than fairy-tale pregnancy, I still couldn't wait to become a mom. My lifelong dream was finally on the verge of coming true. My due date, June 12th, was almost here.

Truth Corner

Looking back, what I remember most is the chaos I felt at each new stage of motherhood. I often had tunnel vision and was in a constant, sometimes debilitating state of crisis and fix-it mode. These days, I have more clarity. I wish someone could have told me some of the things that feel so clear to me now. Especially in those moments when I was panicking and feeling stuck and beating myself up for not doing things "right."

This is why, in these Truth Corners, I'd like to share some of what I wish I'd known then. Perhaps you're in a tough moment, too, and wondering if there is an end in sight. Or maybe you feel, as I often did, like you're just going through the motions, getting through each day without being awake to life. Hopefully these learnings from my own life can help.

About pregnancy

Not everyone has a challenging pregnancy, but that was my experience every step of the way, every single day. Honestly, I hated pretty much every single second of being pregnant. I hated how I felt, how I looked, my energy level, my anxiety about everything. I can only remember two enjoyable days out of my entire 41 weeks—and those were only half-days.

In addition to feeling miserable, I also felt guilty for feeling miserable. I was supposed to be completely excited and joyful about this lifelong dream coming true! I wish I could go back to that time as my present self and speak to my then-pregnant self and let her know that there was a light at the end of the tunnel. I would tell her it's okay to feel the way she feels and to try to focus on the little things that could bring a tiny spark of joy into my life each day.

Here are a few more things that helped me through those days or that might have made my journey a little easier:

Practice Self-Love Affirmations

Affirmations were especially helpful when I was feeling disgusting with my head in the toilet. Here's one I liked:

I am amazing, I am creating new life, I am beautiful, I am whole, I am complete, It's okay to feel whatever way I'm feeling right in this moment. All emotions are okay! They are messages for me.

Make a Plan

If you're having a nausea-filled pregnancy like me, carry vomit bags, crackers, wristbands, ginger candies, Zofran, whatever will help you get through moments of queasiness. Stock your car, office, parent's house, partner's car along with the giant tote of goodies you'll be carrying everywhere with you. I wish I'd given myself permission to use public restrooms instead of trying to get home to throw up.

Tune in to Your Needs

Get conscious. Practice tapping into your needs in each moment. It often helped me to ask myself: "What does Susanna need right now? What does self-care look like for me today? In this moment?" And then listen to those answers. Follow through with the "to do" of it.

Chapter 2

MY DUE DATE came and went. I read and re-read the pregnancy bible *What to Expect When You're Expecting,* trying to find clues and hints that would lead me to the answer I was looking for: when would I finally go into labor? One of my closest girlfriends Latarsha called me up to say, "We're going to Caioti Cafe right now for the 'labor salad.'" Legend was that women went into labor within 24 hours of eating it. I scarfed down the salad and ordered one to go for dinner.

It didn't work.

I stepped on the scale and cringed. I was 50 pounds up and still not finished yet. "Come on!" I encouraged the kicking baby in my uterus, "Aren't you bored in there?" My impatience was growing daily, but I didn't want to begin a relationship with my daughter where her life revolved around my convenience.

I awoke with a jolt on Father's Day morning, 2006. I felt like something was about to erupt in my body. I ran to the bathroom just in time for my water to break. Amniotic fluid gushed everywhere. It was time!

My contractions came hard and fast. I was grateful for both the 5 a.m. hour and empty roads as Brian sped us to the hospital. My clothes and the three towels I was sitting on were soaking wet as fluid continued to flow from my body. I tried to breathe and revel in the moment, but the pain was intense. Any thoughts of having a drug-free birth left my mind completely.

At the hospital, I grabbed the first nurse I saw. "When can I get my epidural?" I asked in desperation.

She smiled gently and encouraged me to relax. "Don't worry, you're still in the early stages." When she checked my cervix, I was only three centimeters dilated. Seven more to go.

Shortly after, I was set up in a labor and delivery room, and the epidural was administered. I was finally able to relax while still feeling the ebb and flow of the contractions.

The next few hours were a blur. Family members started showing up, taking turns to visit us in the delivery room. I was laboring naturally at my own pace.

Although my ob/gyn had been a gem throughout my pregnancy, delivery day was a different story. He was frustrated with his Father's Day golf game being interrupted, annoyed with extra nurses being in the room, and impatient, asking for another dose of Pitocin to be administered. "I'm not on Pitocin," I reminded him. "My birth plan was to labor naturally. Aren't I doing that well on my own?"

I still wanted to stick to my birth plan, but it was hard not to feel the doctor's impatience. When it was finally time to start pushing, I felt pressure to make it happen quickly. But it was hard and painful and my body was exhausted. I was crying with frustration, but somehow I was even more worried about my doctor being upset. After an hour and a half of active pushing, he pulled out a vacuum which he placed at the crown of our baby's head. He pulled with such force that blood spurted everywhere, specks of it landing on his glasses. Brian would tell me later that it looked like a war zone where I had just fought the biggest battle of my life.

As my baby spilled out of me, a piercing cry filled the room. She was so big. And long. Brian cut the cord. The nurses whisked her away and started cleaning things up. She was measured and weighed and tested. She got a few shots. Throughout, she was screaming heartily. "Baby's got lungs!" said the nurses. It's always a good sign when a baby is crying at birth, right?

It was a feeling like no other: the elation in that moment I became a mother. I loved my daughter immediately and fiercely. I wanted to protect her with every cell of my being.

The nurses were done with their poking and prodding. I reached out for my clean and tightly-swaddled baby. She had dark brown eyes. A tuft of dark hair was showing from underneath her newborn hat. She was completely alert and looked at me intently. "Hi, my baby girl," I whispered, with tears filling my eyes. "I'm your mama."

I was over the moon as we introduced our daughter, A., to the family at the hospital that day. I felt like such a successful mother already! I had made it through the birth. A. latched on to my breast for her first feeding and sucked like a champ. The hard part was over.

I stayed at the hospital for two and a half days, but I probably only slept a total of two hours. I didn't realize I would be in so much physical pain with a natural birth, but I could barely walk and needed ice packs everywhere.

When we finally got home, my mother spent the first week of A.'s life living with us and helping out around the clock. I felt a new respect and admiration for her and never wanted her to leave.

But after a week, my mom went back to her duties at

home and my husband returned to the office full time. I was alone with A. for the first time. Reality started to set in. I felt a lump in my throat as I started to think about the looming week ahead. How was I going to do everything by myself? Physically, I was still in a lot of pain. I had stitches from vaginal tearing while giving birth. I had painful hemorrhoids from pushing so hard. I couldn't sit comfortably unless I was on a donut pillow and even then I had to keep shifting around. It didn't matter much anyway, because A. never let me sit for more than a minute. She needed to be held constantly. She also craved constant motion, which meant I was always walking or bouncing her around. In order to get anything done around the house, I put her in a baby wrap so I could be hands-free. I did everything with her strapped to me.

Even then, A. still cried every day from sun up to sun down and I couldn't soothe her. I was overwhelmed with the constant needs of my baby girl. I woke up one day and actually said out loud, "I am *unhappy*." It felt horrible to admit it. Hadn't my life long dream of becoming a mother come true? I was upset with myself for not being happier. I was even afraid to write about my feelings in my journal because this was such a scary, unfamiliar place to be. Still, I couldn't escape this dark feeling brewing inside of me.

However, I felt competent—if not downright victorious—in one area of motherhood: breastfeeding. A. latched on easily after she was born and became a champion nursling from Day One. It was a calming and enjoyable experience for both of us and became a welcome break from A.'s fussiness throughout the day.

But when A. was three months old she started spitting up excessively after each nursing. I didn't understand what was happening and enlisted a seasoned lactation consultant to help me solve this mystery. Immediately upon observing me feed my baby, she determined that I had an overproduction of milk and was therefore overfeeding my child, which then led to the spitting up—A. was full. But as the lactation expert was relaying this information to me, it was the incredulous look she gave me that hit home the most. "Is your child always this fussy?" she asked. "How in the world do you cope?" Of course A. was screaming and wailing while the lactation consultant was there, just as my baby always did, all day long, but I was used to it by then. Until that moment, I hadn't realized that everyone didn't have the experience I was having. As a new mother, this was all I knew.

A.'s fussiness continued to grow. She was whiny before she ate and gassy and uncomfortable afterward. She constantly fidgeted throughout the night. I was holding her in the kitchen one morning, trying to put breakfast together for myself using my free arm. She had woken up crying eight times the night before. She was screaming and the arm I was holding her with was about to fall off. I snapped, slammed the refrigerator door and yelled out loud, "I can't live like this!" It was so bad. I looked at the clock—it was 6:30 a.m. How would I survive yet another day? I kissed A. on the cheek and apologized, "I'm sorry my baby. It's not your fault."

I held on to a beacon of hope, however: the three month marker. Usually this is when colicky babies start to calm down, due to progressive development of their digestive systems. Our pediatrician assured us that A.'s fussiness would significantly decrease, if not dissipate completely by this time. In my most trying moments and during A.'s extra-challenging days, I looked forward to this milestone.

But when A. turned three months old, her fussiness did not subside. In fact, it stepped up significantly. A.'s discomfort and irritability were at an all-time high, and I wanted to crawl into a hole and never come out.

At least A.'s nighttime schedule provided some slight relief. Things were getting a little better with wake-ups only twice a night for feeding at this point. I had crazy days, but I knew that I could sleep a bit at night. I would put A. to bed around seven and then have about two hours to myself before I headed to sleep, passing out within two seconds of my head hitting the pillow.

After a week or two of a consistent night schedule, the normal routine shifted. Brian told me he had plans to meet up with a friend after work, while A. would be sleeping in her crib in her bedroom across the hall for the first time. Up until that point, she'd slept in a little co-sleeper at the side of our bed and often ended up sleeping in our bed.

I got out my journal, lit a candle, and started winding down for bed. When my usual 9:30 p.m. bedtime came around, though, I couldn't settle. I panicked: what if A. woke up to eat and I didn't hear her? I tried to soothe myself, "Everything will be okay. Of course you'll hear your daughter's cries."

But then it was 10:30 p.m. and I was still wide awake. Brian wasn't home yet, but I didn't want to call him and seem needy. I was much more comfortable dealing with my own unmet needs than I was with asking for help. I tried to relax some more, but couldn't. I looked at the clock again. It was now 11:45 p.m. A. usually woke up for her first feeding by midnight. Certainly, I shouldn't try to sleep now if she was going to wake shortly.

Midnight came and went. Now it was 1 a.m. and A. still hadn't woken up. I checked on her a million times but she was still sleeping soundly. Around 2 a.m., as I lay on my back staring at the ceiling with my eyes wide open, I heard my daughter start to whimper. I felt grateful for being useful with my useless awake time and quickly grabbed her for a diaper change and feeding. As I was putting her down again, I felt a pit in my stomach.

"I feel alone," I whispered to myself in the dark as I laid there wide awake. It was unfamiliar to feel so completely by myself in this new normal of motherhood. How could I get comfortable doing this? I eventually fell asleep that night, around 4 a.m. A. woke for the day two hours later and I jumped out of bed, moving rotely through my daily routine.

My anxiety continued to increase as did my sleepless nights. My body was completely out of whack. My psychological and emotional ups and downs were dramatic. As A.'s meltdowns continued, mine grew in frequency.

∾

The day came when I finally agreed to hiring a night nurse on a few occasions. She was amazingly nurturing and friendly. Her intention was to help with two things: 1) getting A. on a daily feeding schedule during which she could "learn" to take in all the calories she needed during the day (and consequently sleep through the night on her own) and 2) bring A. to me for feedings throughout the night. Everything else she would take care of: diaper changing, swaddling and getting A. back to sleep. After a few nights, the nurse promised us, A. would be sleeping from 7 p.m. until 7 a.m.

As comfortable as she made me feel, I still had a ball of anxiety in my chest. I did not like being out of control and the thought of someone else taking care of my baby didn't sit well with me. The evening came for the nurse to spend her first night with us. She sat with me while I gave A. her final feeding of the night and then took her into her room, an air mattress set up for her next to the crib.

I remember feeling uneasy as I got myself ready for bed that night. Something seemed off and I couldn't figure out what. I was exhausted but couldn't seem to feel at ease. All I could think of was A. asleep in her crib by herself. I kept listening for sounds, but heard only complete silence. I crawled under my covers and got ready for sleep. The plan was for the nurse to bring A. to me when she woke up for her first feeding, sometime around midnight. It was already 10 p.m. and although my body was exhausted, I could not turn off the thoughts and worries in my head. Every time I would start to close my eyes and drift off, I would wake with a start in anticipation of A. being brought to me for her first feeding.

I did not sleep a wink that night. I could not relax my mind for one minute while the night nurse was there. My heart was racing and I was sweating. I looked at Brian snoring peacefully next to me. Why was sleep evading me?

Thus began the horrific journey of my downward spiral into a debilitating depression.

Up until this point, I was miserable and sad but didn't feel clinically depressed. I felt like I was able to function on a daily basis. But when my anxiety kicked in and the battle with sleep began, I started to lose it.

There have been many times in my life where I didn't get as much sleep as I needed: studying for midterms and finals during school, dancing until 4 a.m. with my friends, adhering to hectic work deadlines. But I was always able to catch up by sleeping in on the weekends or going to bed early on the nights I could. I had never experienced such a confusing relationship with sleep as I did in these newborn days.

Nothing made sense. I was beyond exhausted—physically, emotionally and psychologically. Our faithful night nurse came through with her promise: after a few nights of training A. and giving me a feeding schedule to follow during the day, my baby was sleeping through the night, 7 p.m. to

7 a.m. I should have been ecstatic: a new woman, energized and revitalized!

The irony is not lost on me: when my baby started sleeping through the night at three-and-a-half months, I stopped sleeping completely. Even though every fiber of my being was tired, my mind was wide awake 24 hours a day. I dreaded the evenings when I started having to think about sleep, because it never came. Ever.

My ob/gyn finally prescribed Ambien for me. I had never taken a sleep aid before and had instant anxiety about it. That night, I set myself up in the guest bedroom downstairs, far away from A. and from any risk of her waking me up. I used ear plugs and put on a sleep mask. I finally fell asleep for the first time in two weeks. Three hours later, though, I was wide awake with a racing heart and sweaty palms. I panicked. "It didn't work! What's wrong with me?"

My depression set in quickly and heavily after that. My goal each day was to just make it through the day, sometimes each minute and hour. I went to see my acupuncturist and holistic chiropractor. I burst into tears every time I had to explain what was happening. I was losing a pound a day, at least. I kept losing weight even past my pre-pregnancy weight and was nearly skeletal within months of having a child. "Wow, you look amazing! You just had a baby?" strangers would tell me when they saw me out and about with four-month-old A. "It's called the anxiety diet!" I wanted to scream. "You're welcome to try it."

I remember one night thinking, "If I do not fall asleep tonight, I am going to call my mother first thing in the morning, ask her to come get my baby, and check myself into a mental hospital." My holistic chiropractor had called and left a voicemail that evening with a mantra for me to repeat over and over: *I am ready, willing and able to receive peaceful, restful, and rejuvenating sleep.* So I did it. I repeated those words a million times. Somewhere around 4:30 a.m. I finally fell asleep. I woke up two hours later, but that tiny amount of sleep felt like years.

The sleeping streak didn't continue as smoothly as I would have hoped, though. My doctor had prescribed Zoloft for my depression, but it made me feel jittery, antsy, and almost psychotic. I wanted to jump off the roof because I felt like I was crawling out of my skin.

Finally, my doctor realized I didn't need sleep aids or antidepressants and decided to give Ativan, an anti-anxiety drug, a shot. I took it that night and immediately felt normal for the first time in months. I was so excited that I ate a real meal for the first time in weeks. I was down to 115 pounds at this point, a far cry from the 167 marker when I gave birth just a few months prior. My appetite was returning.

Looking back, it's hard for me to comprehend why it took so long for me to be prescribed an anti-anxiety medication. As much as I had explained my symptoms in detail to my ob/gyn practice at the time, they refused to focus on anything other than my lack of sleep. Yes, that was my symptom, but my underlying issues of nightly panic, racing heart, and inability to settle down or shut my mind off were largely ignored.

"If you can't sleep, then you need sleep aids," my doctors repeatedly told me. "You need to sleep and then everything else will fall into place." I was beyond frustrated.

Since then I have learned that postpartum depression can often take the form of severe bouts of anxiety. But for a long time, my doctors didn't seem to understand that anxiety was the root cause of what I was experiencing.

Even though the Ativan was helping me a lot, I still had extremely tough days. Sometimes, if I didn't feel like the Ativan was working quickly enough, I panicked. And there was a lesson here, too, one that would often repeat itself in the coming years: there was no such thing as a cure-all, a magic bullet. Because Ativan was considered to be a highly addictive drug and not meant to be taken every day, I needed to come up with a different daily plan.

I was quickly building up quite a medicine cabinet. I now had a prescription for Ativan, Ambien, and Trazodone, an old-school antidepressant that had a side effect of making you drowsy. The first night I took Trazodone, I realized it was a horrible mistake. I was drowsy, yes, but also extremely antsy. I couldn't fall asleep at all. So around 10:30 p.m., when I was still awake, I freaked out and took Ativan. At midnight, when I still hadn't fallen asleep yet, I freaked out further still and took 10 mg of Ambien. I must have passed out but still woke up at 4 a.m. with a terrible meds hangover.

It was around this time that my friend Angela introduced me to a new doctor. I loved her immediately. She was matter-of-fact and warm and down-to-earth and witty. "You need a plan," she said. "And the next time you have a baby, I'm going on sabbatical."

I embarked on a journey of medication ups and downs. After only a few short weeks of taking Ativan nightly, my body had become dependent on it. My new doctor prescribed an anti-anxiety/anti-depressant called Lexapro to help me wean myself off of Ativan. It took me four long months. I would take Lexapro every morning, increasing my dosage slowly because of my sensitivity to drugs. Then I would take Ativan nightly, slowly decreasing my dosage. Sometimes I would cut my Ativan down too quickly and experience terrible with-drawal symptoms. It was scary and unpredictable. My weight started slowly returning and then suddenly skyrocketed. I gained 20 pounds seemingly overnight.

At last though, I was finally able to exhale a little bit. The

Ativan and Lexapro were mostly doing their job and I could take a breather for a moment. Little did I know that I would need to build up as much reserve as possible for the next big battle in front of me.

Truth Corner

Life with a newborn

As a new mother, I was so annoyed with my consistently-unhappy, miserable self. Why couldn't I ever find joy in anything? I found myself in the deepest pit of depression. I hated myself, but then was extremely hard on myself for hating myself. It was an endless hamster wheel of self-loathing and abuse.

Again, not every new parent has a difficult time adjusting to life with a newborn, but that was my experience. I had an extremely fussy child who demanded my attention around the clock. I was overwhelmed and anxious. I didn't even understand what I needed. Looking back, there are some things that helped and some things that I should have paid more attention to. My tops:

It's Okay to Be a Novice

You don't need to have all the answers. Be okay with learning as you go. Every child is unique, every situation is unique. What you do today might not feel right tomorrow. There are no rules! Know that you are doing your best to take care of this child.

Escape with Your Baby

Give yourself permission to be on the baby's schedule and in their world. "Nap when they nap"—yes, easier said than done, but have you tried it? Can you ignore the pile of dirty dishes in the sink for an afternoon cuddle with your baby? And if you can't, just keep practicing. See what happens.

Do Whatever Is Best for You

What's best for you is best for the baby. What's best for you is best for the universe! If you can't breastfeed, don't stress about it. If your baby is a bad napper and you want to wing it, do it. Block out the noise of everyone else's advice (mom, girlfriends, siblings, celebrity moms) and learn to tune in, tap in, and turn on to what serves you best.

Stop Comparing Yourself

Situations with other moms are never going to be exactly the same as yours. The grass is always greener, so practice shining light on your own perfectly imperfect situation. You got this!

Chapter 3

I CALLED MY MOM the day I started taking Ativan for the first time. A. was four months old.

"Mom," I said, "can you please come spend the night? I'm starting this new medication and I won't be able to breastfeed A. in the morning unless I make sure it's completely out of my system. She's never had a bottle before and I need your support in making sure she'll take one in the morning."

Because of A.'s colicky nature and tummy sensitivities, we decided to start with a soy formula. I was so nervous the morning of my baby's first encounter with a bottle. My mom sat in the recliner and held my swaddled daughter. We heated the bottle up just so. I sat nervously on the bed, watching the show unfold. I didn't know what to expect, really. I thought A. would start crying incessantly over something new and different. My anxiety started to bubble up inside of me.

And then A. took the bottle and gulped it down. She was a pro from the start. I wanted to weep with happiness. My baby girl was flexible! It felt like Christmas morning. I exhaled once again.

Though my battle with medication, sleep, anxiety, and depression continued, I was feeling hopeful about mothering A. Her daytime naps were still sporadic, but she was starting to sleep consistently through the night. And she seemed to be thriving in other areas. At her five-month marker, she was 15 lb 4 oz and 25 ¼ inches long. The pediatrician was thrilled.

But as A. continued to take the formula every day, I started to notice new behaviors. Every time I held her, she would try to rub her face into my arm. She started scratching her face, so we had to keep her nails cut short. She developed a red rash under her neck, stomach and chest. Her fussiness began to escalate to an all-time high.

One night, she went to bed around 6:45 p.m. as usual. Typically, she would sleep for 11-12 hours straight. But this particular night, she woke up at 9:45, 12:30, 1:30, 3, 3:15, 3:30, 5, and 6:15. I chalked it up to teething and gave her some baby Tylenol. But the sleepless nights continued and I started to wonder if it was something else. "Could it be allergies?" I thought.

We called the pediatrician and scheduled an appointment. He immediately sent us to a dermatologist, who prescribed a variety of topical ointments. We rubbed them all over A.'s body, daily, but they brought little relief. Instead her poor body grew raw from her incessant scratching. She scratched up her neck, chin, and face until she was bleeding. We started putting socks on her hands at night so she wouldn't hurt herself so badly.

We went to see an allergist who did a prick test on her back. She was so rashy that it was hard for him to find a "clean" place to do the tests. Turns out she had myriad allergies: dairy, nuts, eggs, garlic, beef, coconut, lentils, sesame … the list continued for two pages. She was even allergic to beta-carotene—she couldn't eat anything that was orange! He prescribed an antihistamine called Zyrtec to administer daily. He also said to give her Benadryl as needed, which turned into daily dosages.

Since A. wasn't eating solids yet and was drinking a soy formula that was devoid of all the foods she tested positive for, I couldn't figure out why her rashes continued to spread all over her body. It was so heartbreaking to see her discomfort.

I started putting her in footie pajamas throughout the day, so as much of her body would be covered as possible and less subject to scratching bouts. When she was in her car seat or stroller, I put socks on her hands. And her stroller was always a short-lived excursion because she would constantly rub her arms up and down its shoulder straps, scratching herself raw.

By eight months old, A.'s rashes had turned into full-blown eczema all over her body. We continued our visits to the dermatologist but were just told to put more cream on her. When I expressed my concern about her increasing skin problems to our pediatrician, he only said, "She'll grow out of it. Her immune system is just getting stronger."

The problem was, she wasn't growing out of anything. Her fussiness was even worse. Her eczema was rampant. In fact, her issues were starting to affect her development. For example, whenever we gave her some tummy time to start the crawling process, she would dig her face into the carpet and shake her head back and forth to scratch it. She never learned to crawl.

When A. turned one, we returned to the allergist and did another panel of testing. "Oh," said the doctor, without much affect. "Looks like she's highly allergic to soy. Not sure why that didn't show up on the last test."

I couldn't believe it. My baby was highly allergic to soy and 90% of her diet was *soy formula*. I started weeping for her. My poor baby was suffering because her first allergy test wasn't accurate. It all seemed so unfair. We started A. on Nutramigen, a hypoallergenic formula, the next day.

It was so interesting to see the physical changes in my daughter's skin. Just as the eczema had slowly spread all over A.'s body, it began to slowly leave her body. It left her neck and chest first, then her legs, then her arms, then her hands. By 18 months old, A. had nearly clear skin. She wasn't taking any allergy medications or topical creams on a daily basis. Her diet consisted of beans and rice, vegetables, fish, fruit and certain meats.

But even as the eczema started to dissipate, we still had our fair share of scary allergy episodes. Once, as I was feeding her a dinner of rice and fish, she started to cough and scratch her face. I noticed a rash starting to spread that quickly turned into big hives. Her lip started swelling and she coughed some more. I poured Benadryl down her throat and raced for her Epi-Pen, which I had never used before.

I guess it was the coughing that scared me the most. She couldn't really tell me how she was feeling yet, so I panicked. I immediately called 911 and told them my daughter was going into anaphylactic shock. They were calm and told me they were on their way. We lived in a high-rise in Marina del Rey at the time. There was a hospital two blocks away. I called 911 back five minutes later, as A. continued to cough and I couldn't figure out how to use the epi-pen. "How far away are you guys?" I screamed.

"We'll be there in about seven minutes," they replied.

"Forget it, I'm taking her to the hospital myself," I said.

I ran out of the door with a shoeless A. in tow. A few minutes later I rushed into the ER with my swollen daughter. "Please help!" I yelled. "She can't breathe! Her mouth is swollen!"

And on cue, A. looked around at the office staff with her swollen lips and started singing, "Old McDonald had a farm, ee-i-ee-i-oh!"

I didn't know whether to laugh or cry. My heart was racing and my adrenaline was pumping. The ER doctor quickly brought us into a room where he confirmed that although her lips had swollen, her throat never did.

I'll never forget that drive home. I was frazzled and exhausted. A. was in a Benadryl haze, contentedly lounging in her car seat. We turned right on to Lincoln Blvd., but somehow I missed the sign that said, "No right turn on red." Sirens greeted me quickly and I pulled over. The officer came to my window and before he could say a word, I burst into tears. "Please sir," I said. "We've just come from the ER. My daughter had a pretty bad allergy attack. Have mercy on me?"

He looked in the back seat at my daughter's puffy face and softened. "Yes ma'am," he said. "You take care now." I drove the remaining five minutes home with tears streaming down my face. My daughter was okay! She was going to be okay.

There were so many terrifying allergy episodes over those first few years. It wasn't just specific foods we had to avoid feeding A.; we had to be extremely conscious about cross-contamination as well.

At restaurants, we had to be constantly mindful about the food around us. We always brought A.'s special meals and put everything on "tabletoppers"—plastic stick-on placemats that would cover up the table. Still, there would inevitably be cheese or dairy products left on the arms of chairs or smeared on the back of a booth by a toddler before us. A. only had to touch something she was allergic to to be affected immediately. First, she would start sneezing. Then she would start scratching her eyes. Soon, hives and rashes would pop up and, lastly, her eyes would start to swell shut.

When this happened, we would wipe down her affected areas with a wet cloth and give her Benadryl immediately. Sometimes, though, it didn't kick in for half an hour or more. By then, we would have a swollen-faced child who had become drowsy from the medicine. She was uncomfortable and out of it. It hurt my heart to watch, but we were determined to give her a normal lifestyle. We also held the belief that exposing her to various allergens might strengthen her immune system. I still don't know if that was the right thing to do or not.

∽

When A. turned two, we threw a birthday party for her at a local park. I ordered a delicious cake for all of the guests and made a special allergy-free one for A. As she was blowing out the candles of her special cake, her arms grazed the frosting (dairy! eggs!) of the bigger cake not meant for her. She immediately broke out in hives. And, as it was her custom to start wiping her eyes as soon as her allergy symptoms began, her eyes began to swell shut. So instead of celebrating, A. spent her 2nd birthday party asleep in my arms after a dose of Benadryl.

A few months later, we enrolled A. in a local nursery school where she joined a two-to-three-year-old classroom twice a week. One morning I dropped her off and headed to a cafe to visit with my sister. As soon as I ordered my drink, the school called. "Susanna," they said, "A. is having an allergy breakout, please come pick her up."

I raced back to the school—luckily I was only 15 minutes away. I ran into the classroom and noticed my dear sweet daughter standing by herself in the corner. The teachers were assisting other kids and my daughter was left completely alone. I walked over to where she was—not complaining, not whining. She was suffering silently, trying to deal with her allergy outbreak on her own. She looked up at me and my heart shattered into a thousand pieces: her eyes were completely swollen shut and the rest of her face was covered with rashes and hives. I was so furious with the inattentiveness of the teachers. I swooped up my baby girl and started our wipe down and medicine routine. Then I took her home and cuddled her for the rest of the day. I couldn't believe she didn't cry or fuss. The harsh reality was that she was getting used to these outbreaks.

I became hypersensitive to all of the foods around A. that could trigger her allergies. I had to educate her teachers and caregivers from early on. A child had only to eat a cheese stick and then touch a toy and it would be contaminated. I'm sure this is what happened that day at her nursery school—she must have touched a toy that another kid had touched with their cheese-puff fingers.

I learned all of this the hard way but it soon became second nature. As I was cooking in my own kitchen, cracking eggs for omelets or sprinkling shredded cheese on a tortilla, I learned that I had to thoroughly wash my hands before touching any food for A.

I hated being so anal and controlling with my family members when we went to visit them, but the repercussions could have been dangerous. "Mom," I would say, as she would crack an egg and loosely wipe her hands on a nearby dish towel before handing A. a rice cake. "You have to wash your hands every time you touch something A.'s allergic to!" I'm sure I was annoying, but I had to be so vigilant about this.

Once, while on a family reunion trip to a rented house in Vermont, I discovered one of my sisters using A.'s frying pan. We always traveled with our own special set of pots and pans, along with separate sponges to wash them. When I saw her making an omelet in A.'s pan, I screamed at her. She was shocked and remorseful, and I felt bad for being so dramatic about it. But the repercussions for my child's health could have been fatal.

Over time, A.'s allergies have continued to plague her. She got tested at least once a year and sometimes twice in the early days. People always liked to give advice. "I'm sure she'll grow out of it," they'd say. The reality is, A. is still allergic to a lot of the foods she was allergic to in the first year of her life. As she has grown older, her immune system has strengthened, so she seems to be more tolerant when she is exposed to allergens. Her outbreaks are less frequent and more manageable. But they are still scary.

The amazing thing about A.'s allergy journey is that she learned from an early age to become a strong advocate for herself. To this day, she still asks what the ingredients are in the foods around her. She double checks before she takes a drink of milk: "Mommy, is this oat milk? Are you sure?"

Truth Corner

Having a child with allergies

The thing is, I didn't know I had an allergy kid at first. I just thought I had a fussy, itchy, irritable kid. But turns out, there was a reason for all that. I had to become an advocate for my child and educate those who did not understand the seriousness of her condition, even if I was afraid they would think I was an annoying nag. Looking back, I see how much I have learned and also a few things I wish I'd done a bit differently. Isn't hindsight always 20/20?

Remove the Guilt

Don't wait as long as I did to try hypoallergenic formula or alternate feeding methods! I was so hard on myself (are we noticing a theme here?) about breastfeeding and my ability to give my child life. Hello, I already gave my child life by carrying her in my uterus for 41 weeks! I was so worried about being a perfect new mom, and I knew that one of the most important ways to be a perfect new mom was to breastfeed exclusively for months and years. So when A. was suffering from colic, I didn't hesitate to reduce my own diet in an attempt to make the least offensive type of breast milk for my child's sensitive digestive system. Eventually I was only eating rice and unseasoned ground turkey for every meal. Of course A. still cried incessantly. All that had changed was that I was starving! Then, when I knew I needed medication and that I would have to switch to formula, I was racked with guilt. It took a long time before I could accept that if I didn't take care of myself, I wouldn't be able to take care of A., either.

Be Prepared for Comments

By this I mean to be prepared to respond to the outside world. A. was a child with lots of rashes and eczema early on. It was noticeable to everyone who came across her path. Other people—especially kids and judgmental mothers—always had commentary about my daughter's rashes and skin blemishes. At one visit to the allergy doctor, a place where we expected to find compassion and camaraderie with other families, a mom and her teenage children stared at my 18-month-old daughter with the most incredulous looks of disdain. "What's wrong with her face?" the daughter whispered loudly to her mother, scrunching her own face up into a disgusted scowl.

The mom cringed and shrugged, but she stopped in her tracks when she saw the venom coming through my eyes. "She has allergies, which is why we're here," I said calmly, my teeth clenched.

Have an Allergy Toolbox

Aside from any necessary medications (Benadryl, EpiPen, etc), be prepared for situations with contaminated surface areas like tables, chairs, and toys. Some of the worst allergy outbreaks A. has experienced have been due to contaminated surfaces. I always carried wipes, sanitizer gel, and bottles of plain water in case I needed to do a quick wipe down or to pour over my child's affected area. Tabletoppers—plastic stick-on placemats—were our best friend. This wasn't just for restaurants, this was when we visited family and friends in their environments, and definitely kids' birthday parties.

Chapter 4

I OFTEN REFLECT BACK on the brief moment between the time A. was 18 months and two years old. Sometimes I think of it as my honeymoon period. It was the first time since her birth that she didn't wail if she wasn't held all day. She was on an amazing sleep schedule, going down at 7 p.m. every night and getting up around 6:30 a.m. every morning. Her eczema had started to clear and I didn't have to put socks on her hands to stop her from scratching herself. I had a handle on her allergies (for the most part), and because her skin condition was clearing and she was eating foods she wasn't allergic to, her fussiness subsided significantly. She was walking and talking and calm.

It also felt like she was finally starting to notice the world around her. She loved to be outside. We went for long walks in the marina every day. We went grocery shopping and to Costco and Target. We went to the beach. We explored the library, parks, and museums. I made dinner most nights and waited for my husband to join me on the rare occasion. "Wow," I thought. "So this is what most mothers feel as soon as they have their babies! Okay, so I'm a little bit late to the party, but here I am!" Things felt *normal*.

I was also starting to feel more like myself again. I had successfully weaned myself off of Ativan and no longer needed Lexapro. The 20 pounds I'd gained from Lexapro was also fading away. I did a cleanse and detox. I was feeling cute and energetic. My sleep habits were normalizing. I began to reconnect with my husband. I felt like myself for the first time since I became pregnant many moons prior.

I was also feeling passionate about a new website for parents I'd created. I'd had an epiphany when I was pregnant and wearing an expensive pair of maternity jeans that I'd splurged on. "Hmm," I thought. "I will wear these jeans for a few months until they no longer fit and then what?" I immediately came up with a "craigslist for parents" idea, built it, and launched it. The plan was that families could buy and sell gently-used baby, maternity and kid stuff via the site.

I had just started holding focus groups for the website in my home with new mothers like myself. I wanted to better understand how to market my website to reach them. Up until this point, I hadn't spent a lot of time with other moms and their babies. Most of my friends didn't have kids yet and A. wasn't yet enrolled in school. My attempts at going to "Mommy & Me" yoga classes and the like were always short lived because A.'s temperament wouldn't allow us to sit still in any kind of group setting.

These focus groups became my first chance to get to know other moms and their toddlers. And as I got to know them, I began to realize that A. was a little different. I couldn't pinpoint it exactly and found it hard to describe. I just felt that my child wasn't like the other kids her age.

For example, A. never crawled as a baby but started walking on her own when she turned a year old. Because of this, she never built her upper body strength and could not pull herself up to walk. And if she fell down, she couldn't get back up on her own. Every time A. wanted to walk, I had to put her on her feet. Every time she fell down, I would have to pick her up and put her back on her feet. Little did I know that this could be a red flag in the development world.

But even as my sense of A.'s differences grew, her periodic checkups seemed to prove that I had nothing to be concerned about. These pediatrician appointments marked off all kinds of checklists to track her development. As far as milestones went, A. was right on par with other kids her age. She talked early (and in Spanish!), took her first steps at exactly 12 months, rolled over and sat up when she was supposed to. What was I worrying about? My child was fine.

A few steps away from our high-rise condo complex in Marina del Rey was a cute little nursery school called Kids Pointe. It was sweet and convenient and had no frills. I loved it immediately. I met with the director after A. turned two, and we decided it would be a good idea to enroll her in the youngest classroom with mostly two-year-olds for two mornings a week. My biggest concern was A.'s food allergies. But it was only for a few hours and I would be just five minutes away, so that made me feel more comfortable.

A.'s first official school experience seemed to go well. She enjoyed going every Tuesday and Thursday morning and the teachers were warm and friendly. The school also didn't have strict rules about potty training, which I appreciated. A. wasn't remotely interested in going to the bathroom on her own at this stage and I didn't want the external pressure of making her do something she wasn't ready for.

Sometimes I would come a little early to pick up A. and was able to observe her in the yard or in the classroom before she saw me. Again, I began to notice ways that my daughter was different from the other kids her age. When the teachers called everyone back into the classroom, she was often the last one on the yard, running around in her own world, doing her thing. The teachers would always have to physically prompt her to come back to the classroom, and only then would she comply. During circle time or any period where the teacher was instructing the kids in a group setting, A. would be tuned out, sometimes walking around, absorbed in other things. She often found her way to a rocking horse or stuffed animal. It was hard for her to sit still for any length of time.

I began to realize that A. never responded to my requests or directions either. I remembered a book my mom had handed me when I was pregnant, a tattered, bookmarked paperback: *Your Strong-Willed Child.* "I needed this when I was raising you," my mom had said. Back then I had lovingly rolled my eyes. Hadn't I been a perfect child? But was she right? Maybe A. was just stubborn?

One of the first things that pediatricians check for in tracking a child's development is speech and language processing. So if your kid talks early, doctors tend to disregard the other questions on the test. This was certainly the case with A. She talked early and *a lot.* She spoke with great clarity and articulation from the age of nine months onward. The test also has a huge emphasis on expressive language, and A. was 100% expressive with her speech and language skills.

A. started talking in full sentences early on as well. I never had to wonder what she was thinking, because she would always tell me very clearly. "Mommy, I want salmon and rice for lunch. And chips. And a drink," she would explain. Clearly her speech skills were advanced. But how come she could tell me what she wanted every day—all day—but she would not respond to me when I needed something from her?

I worried that she might not be responding because

something was wrong with her hearing. So I conducted my own little tests. I would go out to the living room while she was in her bedroom and say different things to see if she would respond. "A.!" No response. "Come to mama!" No response. "A., come play with me." No response. "A., time to take a bath." No response. "Cookie!" A. would come running.

It didn't seem like she had hearing issues since she did respond, just selectively and infrequently. Plus, her vocabulary was growing rapidly by the day. How could she learn all these new words if she hadn't heard them somehow in the first place? But if it wasn't her hearing, why didn't she ever look in my direction when I simply called her name?

I started paying more attention to our communication patterns. If she wanted something, she would tell me and I would respond. If I wanted something from her, she would never respond. Then I started noticing that when she wanted something from me, she would just be in her own little world asking for what she wanted. She wasn't necessarily coming to find me, making eye contact with me and making her request known. It was usually me hearing this little voice in the other room listing what she wanted and me running to meet her needs.

I realized that I was never confident about how A. would participate in things. I never expected her to be consistent in her engagement with me or others. It was such a strange conundrum: this seemingly brilliant child could spew out every thought in her head and share all the desires of her two-year-old self, but she was so disconnected from everyone around her, including me.

As I observed my daughter day in and day out, I began to notice more. The way she played with her toys was very interesting. She had a few favorite stuffed animals and loved them dearly. But she did not create scenarios or engage her toys in interactive play. Instead, she would pick up a handful of stuffies and run them from one place in the house to the next. For example, she would run into the bathroom with a handful of plush animals, stuff them in a drawer and leave them there for a while. Then, she would take them from the drawer and go to another room where she would stuff them behind a pillow or on the counter near the toaster. It was so odd to me, but she seemed perfectly content and on a mission as she played with her toys in this way.

⤚⧽

I started to worry about leaving A. at the preschool by our house. It wasn't just because of the one day I discovered her dealing with a terrible allergic reaction all alone. Her lack of social interaction and engagement worried me. I was beginning to wonder if my child was getting anything out of her time there. Did the staff and teachers know what my daughter needed? Was this really the best place for A., or was I just trying to make it work so I could reassure myself that everything was fine?

It was around this time that I got a phone call from one of my sisters who had a few young children of her own.

"Susanna, I've been thinking a lot about A.," she said. "I don't know what it is, but there's something different about her."

I was stunned. And scared. But I also knew that she was right. Sitting with the unknowns around my child's development, and with my sister's prompting, I decided to call my pediatrician. Initially, he tried to calm my fears.

"Don't worry," he said. "A. is developing well, there's no cause for alarm."

But when I started sobbing uncontrollably into the phone, he softened.

"Okay, let me refer you to a developmental pediatrician—perhaps it will ease your mind."

Having the contact info for a certified professional in the area of child development helped a little. I just wanted to feel like I was doing something. I wanted to know that I was moving forward in solving the mystery that was my child. I knew I didn't have the answers myself, so I was looking for someone else to fill in the blanks.

As I came to experience over and over again in these early days, there was always a long waitlist. When I called the developmental pediatrician, I was told that he wasn't taking any new clients. The receptionist must have heard the desperation in my voice, because she kindly referred me to Dr. Anshu Batra, another developmental pediatrician. I called their office immediately and gladly took the next available appointment—scheduled for six months out.

Later, when I was also referred to the Westside Regional Center, a government agency that provided access to services and support for people with developmental disabilities, it was the same thing. I was so uncomfortable when I made my first call to the Regional Center. I didn't really know what to say other than I thought my child might be different and that I was referred to them for an evaluation. Of course, knowing what I know now, I would have emphasized my worries and concerns. I would have underlined all of the red flags around A.'s development. I would have created much more urgency and demanded to be seen as soon as possible. But because I did not know that I needed to do any of this, the Regional Center only reluctantly agreed to an evaluation and then scheduled it for four months out. Not knowing any better, I just accepted this as how things should work.

While I was waiting for our appointment with Dr. Batra to arrive, I also managed to get a referral to Rebeca Bloomfield, a child development specialist. I was able to get an appointment much sooner with her—only a month away—and waited anxiously for that day to come. When I finally pulled up to her home office, my husband and A. in tow, I worried about what she would think of my daughter. On the one hand, I wanted A. to be on her best behavior. On the other hand, wouldn't it be beneficial for the specialist to see all of the challenges and quirks I was experiencing?

Ms. Bloomfield received us warmly. A. immediately started playing with the toys in her office while she asked Brian and me a number of questions about A.'s development so far. Ms. Bloomfield seemed especially intrigued by A.'s battle with allergies and eczema along with her other health issues. She watched our girl interact with the toys, with us, with her.

After an hour, Ms. Bloomfield looked at us and announced, "Nothing to be concerned about here. Your daughter is normal normal normal. I can understand a few delays with her social interaction because she had so many health issues as a newborn. Many times we see a child with health issues early on not being able to fully participate in the world around them, but once they do it's like that's their starting point. So, I expect A. to develop normally from here on out. She is now able to engage in the world around her because her eczema is finally under control."

As we left Ms. Bloomfield's office, I looked at my husband quizzically. Could that really be it? Was I just overthinking everything? But Brian just looked relieved.

Here's the thing—I really wanted to believe it. I even went so far as to cancel my coveted upcoming appointment with Dr. Batra. I called my concerned family and friends and shared the news: "Everything's fine! A. just needs to play a little catch up." When I told my sister that I'd canceled our appointment with Dr. Batra, she seemed concerned.

"You don't want a second opinion?" she asked.

"Oh I'm good! No need to waste more money," I told her confidently. I hadn't learned yet to trust my intuition, to pay attention to it first and foremost. Instead we all resumed our daily routines, and I eased back into what I told myself was our perfectly typical life with A. But something was still nagging deep within me, and each day, it grew bigger. Could Ms. Bloomfield have been wrong?

They say that discomfort encourages you to make a change. And this gut feeling inside of me was extremely uncomfortable. Finally I called Dr. Batra's office again. But this time the receptionist apologized and told me that they were completely booked and no longer taking any new clients. I was about to give up, defeated, when something within me rose to the surface. It was a warrior spirit in me, refusing to be without answers any longer.

"Please," I implored. "I had an appointment with Dr. Batra scheduled for last month, but I canceled after I thought everything was okay with my daughter. Turns out it's *not* okay. I need help and I don't know where to go or what to do. Please, can you help me? I don't know where else to go!" Tears were streaming down my cheeks.

My plea for help worked. The receptionist fit us in for an appointment a month later. I knew I needed answers and now knew that I would not let anyone stop me from finding them, whatever they were. I had a sense that a battle was coming and that I would be on the front lines. It was time to get my armor ready.

Truth Corner

Getting help for your atypical child

If you are having a strong gut feeling that there is something different about your child, take a deep breath, sit in stillness for a moment, and really tune in. If I had the chance to do it all over again, that's what I would tell myself. Instead I kept trying to ignore my gut feeling and act like everything was fine. I also intervened constantly whenever A. and I were in public. I redirected her physically, answered questions posed to her, and guided her to act as if she were tuned into the moment. Of course I knew that she wasn't, but I didn't want other people to know. I created a fantasy for myself that she was an independently functioning child even though the reality was that she needed a lot of prompting, intervention, and help. It was hard for me to admit this even though my gut was trying to tell me the truth. It was only when I started trusting myself that I was able to push for answers and learn more about what my child needed.

Observe and Describe

Keep a journal where you can write down experiences and situations where you've had a question about your child. All things, big or small—write them down. Is there behavior that seems questionable? Do their reactions to situations seem over the top? Do they not seem to be affected by things that should be taken more seriously? Do they have any interesting habits, rituals, or rigidities?

Call Your Doctor

Typically the first call should be to your child's pediatrician or primary doctor. But be a squeaky wheel. Emphasize your worries so that they take you seriously. Let them know how concerned you are.

Push for an Assessment

Gather as much information from professionals about your child as possible. Insist upon some type of assessment—first with a pediatrician and then possibly with a developmental pediatrician, specialized therapists, or your local regional center. Get referrals from other families who have gone through similar journeys. Stay connected to the assessment process with each provider. Ask questions, take notes and make sure you understand the results of each assessment.

Call a Team Meeting

If your child is currently enrolled in a school setting, schedule a meeting with their teachers and administrators to express your concerns. Get their honest feedback. Let them know that you are seeking outside assessment and loop everyone together when more clarity about your child's needs are revealed.

Chapter 5

TO THIS DAY, I do not know how I got through our evaluation at the Westside Regional Center. The assessment area was a bare-walled, lifeless room devoid of anything childlike. The psychologist, Dr. Lawrence, observed my daughter for only a few moments before she turned to me with a frown and said, "This looks a lot like autism. But you already knew that, right?"

"No," I answered weakly. "That's why we're here?"

I wanted to punch the psychologist in the face, grab my daughter, and run far away from that joyless room. Every time the doctor didn't get an acceptable answer from A., she was quick to point out, "Oops! Mom, she failed that one too!" My heart ached as I watched my precious daughter struggling to make sense of her purpose in that room with a stranger she didn't understand.

The psychologist handed A. a doll and a hairbrush and asked her, "What do you do with the comb?"

"Excuse me," I interjected. "A. has never heard the word 'comb' before. I'm not sure she'll understand what you're saying." The doctor seemed unconcerned. The test was making A. miserable.

"Mama," she said repeatedly, "I want to go home."

"Soon, Peanut," I replied. "Mommy's here."

When we were finally excused from the testing area, the psychologist walked us out. On the way to the elevator, we passed through a lovely outdoor walkway with lots of tall trees and greenery. A. stopped to enjoy the view. She loved nature and stood for a while, looking at the plants bustling in the wind. I called her name, but she did not answer. The psychologist later wrote in her assessment that A. didn't have the ability to respond to her mother's commands and that she was completely cut off from the real world. I had to disagree. My daughter was literally stopping to smell the flowers. I knew right then and there that no matter what challenges she faced, I would never want her spirit to be squashed.

Our evaluation with Dr. Anshu Batra was the exact opposite of our experience at the Westside Regional Center. She greeted us with immediate warmth and held genuine regard for us during that initial appointment. She let us know that the first visit wouldn't have all the answers for us, but that she would assess A. multiple times before coming up with a plan. She was smiling and engaging and made us feel at ease immediately. Brian and I sat on a couch in her office while A. played nearby with a plethora of toys.

We were there for two hours, and Dr. Batra asked lots of questions and listened intently. She also had a natural and easy way with A. She laid down on the floor and started playing with her, working on getting organic eye contact and connection from our little girl. It was mind blowing to see A. come out of her shell for these brief moments.

Dr. Batra believed that A.'s physical health issues had been like a fog clouding her development up until that point.

Although our daughter had learned language and vocabulary, she hadn't picked up the corresponding social aspects like communication and interaction. Dr. Batra told us it was just a matter of going back and filling in the gaps in these areas that weren't yet developed. She estimated that A. was about a year behind in social development but on time or even advanced in other areas. She also pointed out that sensory issues were a big part of the picture: A. liked her space, didn't want to be touched, and avoided certain textures.

Dr. Batra explained that the beauty of it all was that the social stuff could be learned. "It's all treatable!" she said with heartfelt optimism and sincerity. When I began to cry, Dr. Batra said, "I hope those are tears of joy!"

Dr. Batra gave us the numbers of an occupational therapist and a speech therapist to discuss initial assessments, and also suggested that I visit a special education/therapeutic preschool in Santa Monica. I felt so much lighter walking out of her office that first day. I had a peaceful sense that we were finally on the right path.

We were scheduled to return for another observation the following week. During that second meeting, Dr. Batra remained upbeat and optimistic about A.'s future. She began to talk to us more specifically about something called "sensory processing disorder." She explained that this meant A. was not processing sensory information in a way that would allow her to provide appropriate responses based on what was going on in the surrounding environment, but that various therapies could help. She reminded us that A. was still young enough to benefit dramatically from these early interventions.

A few weeks later, Brian and I met with Dr. Batra again to receive a diagnosis and specific treatment plan for our child. I had been nervous about the meeting for days. As warm and nurturing as Dr. Batra was, we were still talking about our child and her myriad challenges and needs. It was an emotional topic and I wasn't sure I was ready to hear any "bad" news. I tried to remind myself to keep my intention to enjoy *all* of my life—even the imperfections and hard parts. I knew that in some ways this might be the end of the world as I knew it, and I wanted to be ready to face that change with joy and peace. I wanted my journey with A. to be one where my ears and eyes would remain open and I would stay present. I knew that too often I was just focused on the future, and then I would have intense regret for not living in the moment.

As we entered her office, Dr. Batra was smiling and bubbly, in her usual joyful demeanor. She began by talking about all of the things A. did so well. She then went on to discuss her diagnosis of sensory integration dysfunction and once again told us that A.'s challenges were "fixable" and that she would recover and function normally in life.

Dr. Batra then talked about getting funding for A.'s therapies, something she was extremely passionate about. She said that we might need to emphasize A.'s "autistic-like behaviors" to receive financial support. In retrospect, this was probably just a gentler way to let us know that our daughter was on the Autism spectrum.

We went over our treatment plan, which included occupational therapy three times per week, speech therapy two times per week, and enrolling A. at a therapeutic preschool three mornings per week. At this point, Dr. Batra looked at me and said, "You know, Susanna, this is going to be a full-time job for you."

I already knew, and I was ready. I couldn't believe how life had turned out exactly as it needed to. Brian and I had planned ahead for me to stay home with A. after she was born.

We budgeted accordingly. I couldn't imagine what life would have looked like if we hadn't had this plan in place.

Over the next few days, the reality of A.'s new diagnosis started to sink in. Though it was hard to learn that my child wasn't neurotypical, I was also fueled by the idea that I had a job to do, and that was to fix my child. I would be a Warrior Mama. And if there was someone born for the task, it was me. How I needed this new project! My half-Asian, Capricorn, strict-upbringing heart began to soar. I had a new focus and *this* would become my revival.

Truth Corner

Getting comfortable with being uncomfortable

Being uncomfortable was and is still especially challenging for me. I was an awkward, gawky, nerdy child growing up. It didn't help that my parents worried that all my desires for an active social life were too "worldly" and put restrictions on them.

I always vowed that when I finally became a mother, I would give my daughter permission to be whoever she wanted to be. I would let her go to the movies with friends, dance to secular music, wear lip gloss and hairspray! But the truth was, when I imagined giving my daughter permission to be her true self, she was always unique in a cool way, like some character from "The Breakfast Club." She was everything I'd always wished I'd been as a child. I never imagined that I might have a daughter who was even more awkward than I ever was, who might be quirky or misunderstood or looked at with disdain or confusion. And I certainly never imagined how uncomfortable that might make me feel.

In my journey to understanding how to support A. to be who she is, not who I'd imagined she would be, I've had to get more comfortable with feeling uncomfortable. It hasn't been easy for me, but here are some things that have helped.

Take a Breath

First things first: take a breath. Take a really long, intentional inhale. Be in the moment, breath in every ounce of air you can hold. Then hold it for a few seconds longer. Open your mouth now and gently start to exhale. Take your time. Slowly let the air release from your body, out through your mouth. There's no rush. Slow down. Now repeat the slow inhales and exhales a few times until you start feeling the calmness take over your body. Then repeat to yourself: everything will be okay. Everything *is* okay. Try to stay in the moment, breathing in and out.

Get into Your Child's World

Think about what makes your child tick. Try to get into their world. Who is this precious soul who has chosen you to be their parent? What brings them joy? What causes frustration and upset? If left to their own devices, what would their preferences be? Do they love to be in their own world? Do they want to talk about the same things over and over? Do they want to line up their toys from the kitchen to the back bedroom? Do they want to read in the corner? Do they want to look out the window and watch what's going on outdoors? Do they want to go to the mall and ride up and down the escalators? For me, I had to lie down on the ground to join in my child's line of sight because it was always so hard for her to look up. When I was on the ground, following her eyes and her movements, eventually she would lock her eyes with mine and I would be invited into her world, even for a fleeting moment. Invest in—and seek out—these moments.

Practice, Practice, Practice

Children with special needs give us lots of opportunities to practice being comfortable with being uncomfortable. For me, the discomfort came from strangers questioning what my child was doing and what my child's intention was. I got so many quizzical looks when we were out and about. Sometimes A. would be spinning or talking to herself or galloping about, oblivious to anyone around her. She would bump into people, run into parking lots and streets, wander dangerously close to strange dogs and people. And every time, I had to exercise my restraint from constantly intervening. Okay, yes, I had to run after her when she was in harm's way or darting into the street, but when she decided to have interactions with other people that didn't make sense, I had to learn how to watch from a distance. She needed to have the experience of how others would react and respond to her. As uncomfortable as it was for me, it was invaluable for her—and for those interacting with her, too.

Chapter 6

I 'VE ALWAYS LIKED being busy. I am my mother's daughter—my mother was always the first one up, buzzing with energy and excitement about the productive day ahead. There was never an idle moment in her schedule; everything had a distinct purpose and specific intention.

Like her, I can't bear to sit around without a set plan either. So when I became a stay-at-home mom, it was hard not to have a scheduled agenda. Sure, my hands were full taking care of A., but my days revolved around responding and reacting to her needs. And because she couldn't sit still for long without fussing and constantly craved movement and stimulation, I felt guilty if I wasn't filling every minute of her day with a productive, educational, and healthy activity. It was exhausting.

So when Dr. Batra gave me A.'s treatment plan, I was energized. Finally we could build a more concrete schedule with a plan for every day! A.'s therapies would help provide a more meaningful structure for her without me having to entertain her every second of the day. And finally I had some tangible tasks to complete!

The first few items on my list were easy: getting A.'s hearing and vision checked by specialists. We visited the ophthalmologist and the ear clinic, and A. was given an A+ by both. Her hearing and eyesight were perfect. Next on the list was an assessment with the speech therapy clinic. After our initial visit, I was called back in for the results. Our two therapists, Erin and Judy, were kind and encouraging. They were mothers themselves and seemed genuinely interested in my sweet little girl. We reviewed the assessment results together and I learned that in cognitive, communication, and social-emotional areas, A. had mild to moderate delays. When it came to receptive auditory processing/communication, however, she had a severe delay. This is why she was often tuned out—she was just trying to cope with all of the sensory input coming her way. She wasn't able to process all of it smoothly. It's like there was a traffic jam in her brain and everything was running into each other and all over the place.

Erin and Judy had a clear sense of how they wanted to direct their therapies and told me that I would be seeing a different child within three months. They were encouraged that A. was still so young and determined that the next six to 12 months would be the most intensive for her. The plan was for A. to come to speech therapy twice a week to work on early stage auditory comprehension and processing skills, expressive language skills, and cognitive skills related to attention, concept development, and play. I felt so encouraged by all of this planning. I couldn't wait for my daughter to start making progress. Okay, so maybe I didn't understand exactly what A. would be working on, but the important thing was that we had our speech therapy plan. I checked it off my list.

Next up on the list was occupational therapy. I remember driving A. to her first appointment. She was singing in the back seat while I wondered what an occupational therapist was exactly and how they could help my child. Wasn't this someone who helped people do their jobs better? Or placed them in the right job? I was clueless.

A woman dressed in a colorful print greeted us in the waiting area. "Hello! You must be Susanna and A.," she said in a sing-songy voice. I liked her immediately. A. seemed comfortable and at ease, too. She led us to a big therapy gym full of swings, a ball pit, and countless things to climb and jump on. If I was a kid, I'd feel like I was in paradise. A. ran right in.

Aneeta Sagar started her first treatment with my child as I sat nearby. At first, it just looked to me like they were playing. Aneeta was swinging A. on a tire swing back and forth. Then they played catch with some bean bags. "I could do this," I thought, "and for much less than $165 an hour." But as the session went on and Aneeta and A. got more comfortable with each other, I realized there was a method to everything that was happening. Aneeta later explained to me that everything she was doing would help regulate A.'s sensory systems. Then she introduced me to two sensory systems I had never heard of before—proprioceptive and vestibular. Proprioception is sometimes referred to as the sixth sense and it helps us sense where our body is in space. The vestibular system helps us keep our balance and coordinate our movements and is also involved in emotional regulation. I was quickly learning that there was a lot more to occupational therapy than I had imagined!

The last item on my list was to enroll A. at an early intervention therapeutic preschool for a few days a week, a few hours at a time. Thankfully, A. was eventually able to receive funding for this—if not, it would have cost the impossible sum of $75 an hour. I began the enrollment process even before we had the funding because I was so eager to get started and desperate for the life-changing help—I relied heavily on my faith that everything would work out financially.

There were a number of preschool programs sponsored by the Westside Regional Center to choose from, but Step by Step in Santa Monica was the one that immediately felt right for us. The owner, Shelly Cox, had a special-needs daughter of her own, and Step by Step was a labor of love, inspired by her own need to find a school for her child.

I remember talking to one of the teachers at Kids Pointe on A's last day there. I explained that she would be attending a therapeutic school so she could receive early intervention for some of her needs. I was feeling optimistic and told the teacher how I was looking forward to getting A. some specific help. "It will be so beneficial!" I said.

The teacher looked at me unenthusiastically and replied, "Well, maybe." It was such a strange comment from a teacher who had not once pointed out anything different or concerning about my child in the months she had been at the school. In that moment I realized I had greater peace of mind now that A. would be enrolled in a more restricted school environment where her teachers would pay increased attention to her needs.

Step by Step was my first experience being a part of a world where A.'s issues were the norm. I never felt like my daughter was in trouble or being "bad," but that instead she was protected and taken care of. The staff was warm, open, inclusive, nurturing, and engaging. I felt like we were forming a solid team around A.

Step by Step was also my first experience getting to know other parents like me. One of the many great things about the school was that they had cameras in all the classrooms and play areas and there was a parent room with monitors where we could observe what was going on. Spending time in the parent room watching A.'s interactions with her teachers and her peers helped me feel connected to her, and also gave me a chance to begin forging friendships with other special-needs parents. A. was making her first friends here, too. I was able to exhale in the presence of other special needs parents and let A. run around in her full quirky glory without embarrassment or shame. I am still friends with many of those moms from the early days. We were all like deer in headlights back then, clueless and naïve about what to do and what lay ahead of us.

Eventually, as I settled into my new routine, my days began to fly by. I was carting A. to speech and occupational therapy four or five times per week. I was also looking into alternative therapies and programs that touted the latest healing in children with similar issues.

I enjoyed being with A. during these sessions. I felt like a student, soaking in so much new information completely foreign to me months earlier. It was fascinating to see A. progress as well, sometimes in very short periods of time.

All week long, I was talking to the therapists about A.'s goals and progress and asking about what other things we could do at home to help things along. I was making gluten-, egg-, dairy-, soy-, and nut-free meals three times a day. I was managing daily meltdowns from A.'s seemingly endless issues with sensory overload.

I was exhausted. But I was also hopeful. I felt like I was finally doing something worthy with my time. I never knew myself to fail at anything, and I was determined that mothering A. would be no exception.

Meanwhile, Brian and I had decided to sell our Marina del Rey condo. So in the middle of all this, I was also trying to keep our place "show ready" at all times, which was impossible with a toddler. Sometimes the realtor would call to request a showing with only a few hours warning. This often meant me scrambling to clean the house and pack up snacks for A. and activities to help keep her occupied for the time we would need to be out of the house. Because of A.'s food allergies, I could never rely on eating out at a restaurant and always had to prepare little containers of A.-friendly fare.

I remember one day when the realtor called with a last minute request for a showing. The house was a disaster but I managed to straighten everything up, get A.'s things together and go. It was rainy and windy, so we needed to find an indoor option. First, we headed to the Marina del Rey library. But soon A. was too loud and disruptive for the staff's liking. After some evil stares, we packed up and left.

My next idea was to take her to a mall with an indoor play area. We went to one, but she quickly grew tired of it, so I drove on to another. At this point, we had been gone from the house for hours and A. was fussy and full of energy. The realtor usually let me know when everything was wrapped up, but I still hadn't heard from him and he wasn't answering my calls. Finally, after six long hours, he picked up his phone. "Are you done? Can we go back home?" I asked.

"Oh, sorry," he said. "The appointment ended up rescheduling for tomorrow. Okay if I come back with them at 10 a.m.?"

This kind of scenario was a common theme in my life at this time because I was always trying so hard to be accommodating. I don't like to rock the boat, so I often found myself acquiescing to others' needs over mine. When I complained to Brian about that miserable day, he responded with a simple question: "Why didn't you tell the realtor that it wasn't a good time?" The truth was that I had never considered the possibility of saying no or presenting a different option. It had not occurred to me that I might have some control over the situation.

This was the start to a very big lesson for me. I had to learn how to take in a request, pause, think about what would work best for me, possibly present an alternative solution, and then ask for what I needed. Of course, this is much easier said than done if you are a people pleaser like me.

Truth Corner

Making the most of your child's therapy journey

In the beginning of A.'s journey into the world of special-needs life, our time was consumed with therapies upon therapies. My entire existence revolved around receiving recommendations for various therapies—and recommended therapists for said therapies—and then scheduling appointments and going to them. Looking back, here are some of the things I learned that helped me keep track of everything and make sure that everyone was on the same page.

Ask Questions

Take notes throughout the week about any questions that come up for you about your child. Even if you're afraid that your questions might be repetitive, annoying, or not that important, write them down anyway. Then either email your therapist before your next appointment or ask your therapist to allocate a few minutes at the start or end of each session to ask your questions and get an update.

Keep Records

Always get copies of any reports or notes your therapist puts together—which they should be doing each session with your child. Carry a notebook where you can keep track of all your questions, updates, and paperwork for each therapist. Save sample work from therapy sessions as well. You never know when you might need all these records for an assessment or funding eligibility.

Collaborate

Work on goals together. Ask for monthly meetings to discuss updates in addition to getting downloads at each therapy session.

Ask for Homework

Most therapists will give you exercises to do at home, but take it a step further and ask for a schedule. Ask for home strategies and get specifics. Talk about this plan as a team with your child present, and bring them into the conversation, too.

Team Work Makes the Dream Work

Make sure everyone on your child's team, from therapists to educators to caregivers, understands the schedule, therapy goals, and any updated notes around your child's progress. It's especially important to let therapists know if there are any external circumstances—like transitions, illness, or lack of sleep—prior to a therapy session so that they can take those extenuating factors into consideration during their treatment.

Chapter 7

I DIDN'T MEAN TO get pregnant again.

At first I felt conflicted about the idea of having another child. Everyone, including and especially the therapeutic professionals in A.'s life, sold us strongly on the idea of how important it would be for A. to have a neurotypical sibling. Dr. Batra even told us, point blank, that we would need a break from focusing solely on A. "Trust me," she said. "You guys need another child."

I'd always wanted to have lots of children, but my experience with motherhood so far had thrown a big wrench in those plans. Still, I wanted to feel like I had explored the option. So I asked other special-needs families about the pros and cons of having more than one child. Most of the time the feedback was favorable. I also noticed, though, that I was meeting more and more families who had multiple children with special needs. This completely floored me. I didn't think I would be able to handle the special-needs journey a second time.

I decided to look into medical studies and research around

having multiple children with autism. I eventually found a top geneticist at UCLA Medical Center and made an appointment with her immediately.

Dr. Barbara Crandall was in her 70s, with a warm smile and stylish white hair. I told her I was worried about having another child on the spectrum and wanted to do some due diligence before even thinking about conceiving another child. She nodded her head in understanding and proceeded to drill me, in detail, about each family member in both Brian's and my family. The questions were thorough and lengthy. After about an hour of this, Dr. Crandall sent me to the lab to get some blood work done. In the end, she didn't have any concerns at all. But, because I was so desperate for hard facts, she finally gave me a number: there was less than 5% chance we would have another child with autism and, in her opinion, more like less than 3%.

But when I thought about it, even the 3% chance that I might be a special-needs mama times two was overwhelming. Then I remembered my family's history of twins. Suddenly my brain spiraled out of control and my heart started palpitating at the thought of being a special-needs mama times three.

I decided then and there that I was done and that it was absolutely enough for me to only have one child.

And yet, here I was, pregnant for the second time.

I felt so guilty for my thoughts. I had girlfriends trying every fertility drug and Chinese herb concoction trying to conceive. Meanwhile, I was pregnant by accident, and it was a miracle I did not want.

I was flabbergasted, overwhelmed, scared, and nervous all at once. I went online and calculated the baby's due date. Baby #2 was due January 3, 2011—on my own birthday. I was going to have a Capricorn and felt 99.9% certain that it was a girl. Was this baby the one destined to be my Mini Me?

That night I barely slept, tossing and turning with anxiety. Sleeping peacefully beside me, Brian didn't seem to be worried at all. He was excited for A. to have a sibling. But transitions were always so hard for me. I was just getting into a groove again. Did I really want to rock the boat? It had been me and A. for so long now and here I was changing things up.

People often say that your second pregnancy will be different than your first. If you had a hard time the first go round, the second would be a breeze. I was banking on these old wives' tales being true. Every fiber of my being still remembered the hell of my first pregnancy.

᷍

Unfortunately, my second pregnancy *was* different than my first, but only because it was ten times harder. I was sick again, but in a new way. It almost felt as if I had some kind of poison coursing throughout my body. I threw up constantly and often found myself laying on the floor, crumpled in an agonizing ball of pain and nausea. Add taking care of a challenging child to the mix and I just about jumped off a cliff. My mother was on summer break and came to help me with A. My youngest sister, also on her summer break from college, flew out from Boston to run errands and cook for me.

On the phone with my best friend Tara, I finally confessed, "I don't want this child, I'm miserable."

"I know," she said, sympathetically. "But there's nothing you can do about it now. You might as well get used to it."

"Well actually, there is something I can do about it," I almost whispered. "I'm only eight weeks along." I paused, my voice becoming quieter still. "I mean, I can still get an abortion."

She inhaled audibly, but then quickly, in true best friend form, responded, "I got your back. Just let me know how to support you."

Had I really said those words out loud? I felt like I was looking at the picture of a beautiful, innocent, cherubic child and screaming, "I do not want you!"

But then, something happened. I saw my baby's heartbeat for the first time. There it was, on the screen at my new ob/gyn's office. A real live heartbeat was inside of me. Life that I had created! I sighed and pictured the looming months ahead. "Maybe it's a sign from God that A. needs to have a sibling," I thought to myself. I left the office with a growing sense of acceptance. So, this is it. I'm doing this again. For some reason, this little soul has decided to choose me to be its mama.

Another feeling crept up on me at the same time: a kind of relief about being pregnant again. I knew, for sure, that after this I would be done with pregnancy forever. Now there was a clear end in sight and I would never have to do it again. I also felt like this would be a more conscious pregnancy than my first; I had been here before. I wrote out a specific intention for my pregnancy: that it would be a peaceful, vibrant, and conscious pregnancy. I felt prepared and ready for the journey.

But I also felt very sick. Heartburn, nausea, and achiness set in right away. I started coughing and had lots of congestion and a sore throat. I was moody and emotional. My anxiety started to flare.

Then A. and I both caught a cold and were coughing nonstop with runny noses and fever. She couldn't go to preschool, so I had her home with me all day without a break, both of us feeling miserable together. Despite my intention, I couldn't help thinking about how much I hated being pregnant. Then I would be racked with guilt. "Sorry little baby," I thought. "I don't want to take this out on you." And then I would hate myself for being so dramatic and whiny and complaining all the time.

I was so detached from my ob/gyn visits for Baby #2 that when I showed up to my next appointment and the doctor started frowning at the screen I wasn't sure how to respond. "Hmm," she said. "The baby's not growing as we would expect. But, I've seen this before—either you'll have a thriving child next week or the pregnancy will dissipate. Hang tight."

I tried to be present in my feelings for the next seven days. There was a 50/50 chance that my baby would make it. My maternal instinct kicked in and I prayed for my baby. "Fight, baby," I said. "Mama will love you so fiercely, little one. Hang in there."

The following Wednesday, my sister Shenandoah drove me to my appointment. I waited for 45 excruciating minutes until my name was called. Dr. Gibbons inserted the ultrasound while I kept my eyes glued to the screen. She found my baby and zoomed in. And, nothing. Nothing was happening. No heartbeat, certainly no movement. And very little growth from the previous week. "I'm sorry, Susanna," she said. "We knew this was a possibility."

"It's okay," I said, with forced optimism.

Dr. Gibbons scheduled a D & C procedure to clean me out. My father drove me to the appointment and I was grateful for his calm presence. The procedure was uncomfortable and I was glad for the effects of the Valium and Demerol. I left the office and found my dad napping in the waiting room. "Time to go, Dad," I said. We walked to the elevator and my tears began to fall. "My dear daughter, I'm sorry," he said, trying to comfort me. I had resolutely determined that I would muscle through the ups and downs of this pregnancy. Now I just felt empty.

I had a period of mourning for the lost baby. I was hit

with waves of sadness throughout the next few weeks. I felt guilty for complaining so much about being sick. I missed my little baby. I wished there was something I could have done to protect her. I was also very emotional about the fact that I would never be with child again—this second time around had absolutely confirmed how much I hated being pregnant. I was not going to do it again.

I was at least looking forward to feeling normal and morning-sickness-free, but that ended up taking awhile to subside as well. So here I was, without a baby, still feeling sick and miserable. I worried that I had zero patience with A. in those days and I felt like a complete failure for not even being able to handle one kid.

Life continued to move forward, but I found myself having more and more "woe is me" moments. Because of A.'s severe food allergies and special needs, I felt like I had to be so hopeful and positive all the time. Deep down, though, I was just worn out. It didn't help that my sleep had been severely affected ever since my battle with postpartum depression. I felt anxious at night and my sleep was constantly interrupted. I was developing dark circles and bags under my eyes.

I was also having anxiety attacks almost daily because we were living in an apartment where our downstairs neighbors hated us with a passion. Every time A. ran across the floor, they banged at the ceiling. Once, I was doing a yoga pose in the living room, lost balance and tipped over to the floor. That incident warranted a visit from the police, one of many police visits in the coming months for disturbing the peace.

One night, I had just finished giving A. a bath and was getting ready for bed. It was 7 p.m. I had cooked dinner and had just taken a fresh batch of chocolate cookies out of the oven. A. was in her zip-up footie pajamas, hair wet and braided, looking at books quietly in her room. Apparently her bath time had been too disruptive, because the neighbors called the police, citing harassment with malicious intent. When I opened the door and saw the familiar faces of the local cops for the umpteenth time, I smiled and sighed.

"Hi officers, looks like you're back again. Would you like some cookies?" I asked.

The two policemen sighed back and apologized, explaining that they had to show up every time a complaint was made.

Soon I found out that our downstairs neighbors were filing a ridiculous lawsuit against us for emotional distress from noise. I knew we would have to find a way to get out of our lease and into a new home, and I felt exhausted thinking about all the work it would take to make this happen and how much of it would fall on my shoulders.

I was so fed up and frustrated, but I also felt guilty for feeling that way. I didn't want to sound like a broken record, complaining and depressed all the time. I wanted to focus more on the positive things in my life. I wanted to relish all of my blessings.

One of those blessings was that A. was thriving with her therapies and preschool classes. Responding to simple questions had always been a big challenge for A. Instead of answering yes and no, A. would just repeat the question. It was a delay in her reciprocal language processing.

One day, on our drive home from Step by Step, I asked A. if she had a good day at school, expecting to be met by complete silence as usual. But instead, after a beat, I heard her small voice answer, "Yes." I held my breath and asked another yes or no question: "Did you have fun with friends?" Again, from the backseat, a quiet but definitive "yes." I was absolutely ecstatic. I asked a few more yes or no questions, and each time A. answered succinctly and specifically. I had to pull over to the side of the road and let the cars behind me pass as tears streamed down my face. My baby girl could answer questions! Her reciprocal language skills were improving and it felt like nothing short of a miracle.

Truth Corner

Dealing with anxiety, worry, and stress

I've always been a worrier. Growing up, I never needed external punishment as motivation. My worries and anxieties about failing to meet expectations were enough to keep me following all of the rules. It was a lot of pressure, though, to feel like I always needed to have my stuff together. I didn't understand how to give myself permission to feel differently. I stressed and worried and let the anxiety take over me. My shoulders were always raised up high and tension in my body was thick at all times. I needed to learn how to breathe and let go, a completely foreign feeling for me. It can still be a challenge for me to do this today, but I've learned a few things that always help me:

Identify Stressors

What triggers the onset of your worry or anxiety? When does your heart race faster? When do you feel out of control? One way to identify stressors is to also notice the moments when all feels peaceful. What's in place when that is happening? Have you slept well? Is your child "happy"? What are the external factors in your life that feel like they are in order or not in order?

Find Ways to Release

What can help you find a release in these moments of worry and stress? Can you write about it? Talk to someone? Take a nap? Exercise? Scream? Hit a punching bag?

What Feels Good?

Make it a priority to identify things that make you feel better. Remember that these can differ in each moment. Find what works for you and add it into your life. Make it non-negotiable.

Remember: Feelings Trickle Down

Your child *feeds* on your feelings. Your anxiety can be contagious! Taking the time to take care of yourself can help you take better care of your child.

Meditate/Pray/Get Quiet

It doesn't matter what word you use to define this kind of quiet time. Just make sure to take a few breaths every day, be present with yourself, call in what you want more of and less of. Ask for your heart's desires! Listen in the quiet moments to what you're here to learn. Silence is golden. Reset yourself.

Chapter 8

I DON'T REMEMBER SCHOOL ever being an issue for me or my siblings growing up. We moved a few times throughout childhood, but always ended up going to the local public schools. I do remember one exception in high school: my parents were impressed with the academic curriculum of another public high school, right outside our zoning area. In order for me to go to that one instead, I had to sign up for German, something not offered at my local high school. Either way, there was never a need for any of us to find schools that better suited any challenges we had.

While pregnant with A., I was certain I would never buy into the parent trap of needing my child's school to define me. We would find an amazing public school for her—after all, I was a fine product of public school education. Of course, none of my perfectly-laid plans included having a child that didn't fit into my mold.

Even though the first four years of A.'s life had been filled with therapies, doctor's appointments, and assessments, and even though the more structured environment of Step by Step had been the best fit for her, I still had not let go of my plan. Neither had Brian. He was certain that our daughter would soon be ready to fit into a neurotypical classroom. So when the time came for us to find the next school for A., we were about to make some big mistakes. I resisted the notion that she might need something different than the plan I had for her. In the end, I would find that maybe I had bought into that parent trap of needing my child's school to define me after all.

A. would be five years old when the fall came around, but we knew that she wasn't quite ready for mainstream kindergarten yet. Still, it wasn't uncommon to give your child the gift of time and start them in a pre-kinder program at the age of five instead, so we felt everything was proceeding according to plan. This just meant that we had to look at various pre-K, developmental kinder and transitional kinder programs at private schools instead of public ones.

I toured a number of schools and I learned so much from each of them, including what would definitely *not* be a good fit for my child. I remember touring one school and walking out 10 minutes into it. When we walked into the pre-K classroom, the only way I could describe what I saw was pure chaos. The teacher looked frazzled and checked out. Some of the kids were wandering in the hallway, unattended, apparently on their way to use the restroom. Another group of students were playing with a bunch of wooden blocks to the side, throwing them at each other and screeching in return.

At the end of the day, we decided to apply to a handful of schools which were lottery picks and one school that had a more in-depth application process. Step one for the Culver Academy was to fill out a fairly lengthy application and then hope to be chosen for an interview.

When we were called in for an interview, it felt like a

victory in itself. This meant that at least on paper we looked good enough to be considered for the school. It was early February when we brought A. in for the admissions interview. We had explained as thoroughly as possible about A.'s challenges and ongoing therapies in the application. Still, Brian and I were nervous, mostly because we knew how unpredictable our child was.

I dressed A. in a cute Ralph Lauren Polo dress and put two bows in her hair. As we walked into the school, A. in the middle holding both of our hands, I thought to myself what a cute family we were—friendly, easy-going, generous. Any school would be lucky to have our patronage.

When the admissions director, Laurel Hamilton, led us into her office, A. looked in awe at the many stuffed animals and figurines of Minnie Mouse around the room. "Do you like Minnie?" A. asked her. She laughed in response, "Yes, I do. How did you know?"

Mrs. Hamilton asked A. a number of questions—identifying colors, numbers, pictures. When it came to the alphabet, Mrs. Hamilton was looking for A. to identify all 26 letters on a chart with associated pictures next to them. What A. did, instead, was not only list each letter in the alphabet but also identify each picture associated with the letter on the chart. Mrs. Hamilton raised her eyebrows, obviously impressed.

Next, she asked A. to draw a picture of a person, and draw A. did. She had never drawn with such precision and detail in her life! She verbalized everything she drew: "This is the person's head and eyes and ears and nose and mouth. Now this is the body with arms and legs—oh and two nipples." Brian and I both laughed nervously, but Mrs. Hamilton just nodded and smiled.

Next, Mrs. Hamilton brought out cards that had numerous pictures of pieces to a greater puzzle. For example, if there was

a card with pictures of sand, waves, and sun, the correct answer
was to label it "the beach." A. was given a card with handle bars,
a bicycle wheel, and a bicycle seat. A. responded directly and
confidently, "It's a unicycle." Truly, there was only one wheel.
Mrs. Hamilton looked flabbergasted in a good way, knowing
the acceptable answer could have easily been just "bicycle."

After the assessment was over, we went on a quick tour
of the grounds. As we walked out to the Pre-K/Kinder yard,
I turned to Mrs. Hamilton and asked, pointedly, "So, what
exactly are you looking for in your assessment?"

"Well, we're looking for a child to be kinder-ready, actually, even when assessing for Pre-K. And A. is obviously ready."
My heart skipped a beat.

Yet at that same moment, I watched my child take in the
playground surroundings and bite her hand. She was anxious about something, I knew. Mrs. Hamilton didn't seem to
notice.

We walked into an empty classroom next. There were lots
of fun toys and creative items for A. to explore. But again, I
saw her biting her hand. I wasn't sure what she was thinking,
but I knew better than to intervene and bring attention to it.

Brian and I left the school with an air of hopefulness.
A. had performed beyond our expectations throughout the
assessment. The stars were finally aligning. I tried my best not
to think about A. biting her hand.

A. received placements through the lottery to the other
schools we had applied to, but when she was accepted to Culver
Academy it meant so much more. "She did it on her own!" I
screamed with excitement. "My baby girl did it!" She had nailed
the assessment questions and breezed through the interview
process. For sure, this school would be just as proud to have our
child as we would proudly be attending. I couldn't wait.

It felt so good to fit in as a parent at a mainstream school.

While attending an evening for new parents before the school year started, I remember feeling thrilled to be so normal. I thought back on the past few years of hard work and financial investment in all of A.'s therapies and interventions. It had really paid off. Now here we were, washing our hands of the special-needs world and moving forward.

I ran into a mom I'd known from Step by Step. "Oh hey!" I called out to my friend. "Is your son coming to school here next year?" "Yes, " she stated, proudly. "A., too!" I squealed. We gave each other high fives, both knowing the intensity of the journeys we had been on with our children thus far. We had made it.

And so I dove into the school year. I participated in all of the activities and fundraisers, grateful to Culver Academy for recognizing the amazingness of my child. After two months, we received our first progress report which read: "A. is off to a great start!"

Sometimes, though, I wasn't so sure. There were moments where A.'s anxiety seemed to be getting worse. Like the time I'd picked her up from school after getting my hair done. Most mornings, I would pull my hair up into a quick bun before dropping A. off and then leave it that way for the rest of the day. But on that afternoon, I'd finally managed to squeeze in a hair appointment. It felt like such pampering to get my roots done! My hairdresser, David, gave me a lovely blow out and I felt beautiful.

As I walked toward the school's pick-up area, I saw A. watching me approach. Her brow furrowed and she bit into her arm—hard and deep. It wasn't a quick bite, either. She dug in with purpose. I could almost see her heart rate increasing with each step closer. "Why is your hair long, Mama?" she asked me, biting her arm again for emphasis. "I don't like it when your hair is long." Was this a sign that things felt out of control to her? That she desperately needed to hold on to whatever felt familiar as much as possible? If my hair changing from morning to afternoon put her over the edge, what were her days at Culver Academy really like?

Our first parent-teacher conference was scheduled for Friday, 11/11/11, and I hoped that it was an auspicious sign for a phenomenal day ahead. Even though we had only heard good things from the school about A.'s time in the classroom, my heart sped up and I felt butterflies in my stomach as Brian and I parked and walked toward the school. I always felt that way when we had to talk to professionals about our daughter. My defenses automatically got triggered and stood at immediate attention. I would take extra care getting ready, imagining that by dressing up and being social, friendly, and over-the-top neurotypical, I would let everyone know that whatever challenges my child had could never be a result of my inept and underqualified parenting.

We walked into Ms. Rappaport's classroom. She was young, petite, and bubbling with energy. A. adored her. As we were about to make small talk about our daughter and the school year and the weather and anything else to avoid the inevitable discomfort of discussing intimate details about our child, there was a small knock on the door before it promptly swung open. There stood Howard Carlton, Head of School and the most intimidating human I have ever met.

I flashbacked to a year earlier when I was visiting Culver Academy for the first time. One of the selling points of the school was that they had the staff and resources to assist with auditory disorders. During a Q & A with all prospective parents, I'd tentatively raised my hand. I didn't know much about hearing impairment and loss, but I did know about auditory challenges. I asked if the school would provide support for my daughter's auditory processing disorder. Mr. Carlton had looked at me coolly and responded that the school accommodated children with hearing impairment specifically and that there were a wide variety of learners at the school. There was something about his dismissive and accusatory tone that made me want to run out of the auditorium right then and there. It was another red flag I had done my best to ignore.

Mr. Carlton walked into the room, smiled at us, and then sat down quietly at the round table. Ms. Rappaport seemed a bit flustered by his presence. Was it ever a good sign that the head of school made a special appearance for your child's conference?

Before Ms. Rappaport could get through the next paragraph in her report, Mr. Carlton interrupted and looked at both of us directly.

"Here's the thing. A. is a very mysterious child. We just don't understand her. We sometimes question her intention in anything she is doing throughout the day. What exactly is her plan? What is she doing and why?" Mr. Carlton continued, "The thing is, she just seems to stand out. She sometimes seems to be wandering aimlessly, without much purpose or direction."

Mr. Carlton went on to discuss their extensive assessment and observation process. Apparently they had been coming to the classroom to check on A. specifically and to determine if she was in the right environment.

I started asking questions, almost becoming accusatory myself. "So you're saying my child is just wandering aimlessly all day? Maybe this is not an appropriate place for her to be if my child has no clue what she's doing." My outburst was met with reassurance that A. was indeed learning and growing and that they were just observing her to try to figure out how to understand this mysterious child.

"Let's reassess in January after winter break," concluded Mr. Carlton. Our parent-teacher conference was over.

I felt betrayed by this private school that happily took our hefty tuition sum but seemingly knew nothing about what our child needed. I was angry that this was the first time we were hearing of any of this despite all the whisperings and conversations that had obviously been happening behind our backs for the past few months. And I was angry at myself. How had I gotten so caught up in this delusion? I had wanted us all to fit into the typical world so desperately that I had ignored all the signs.

Over the next few days, I was in a daze. My bubble had been burst, though deep down I had to admit that I had probably been expecting it. I needed to stop thinking about my own hopes and dreams and start thinking about what the absolute best situation would be for A. I had focused for so long on getting my daughter to "fit in" to a mainstream environment that I had never considered it might not be the best situation for her. I had been told, repeatedly, from Dr. Batra and other therapists, that A. needed to be around neurotypical kids. Now I had a nagging feeling that she wouldn't reap the benefit of being around neurotypical kids until she was *ready* to be around them.

I couldn't stop worrying about my child and what others thought of her. Yes, she was a different kind of kid. And I wanted her uniqueness to shine. How could I support and encourage her to be herself but also help her fit into the world that she was born into? I worried about her inappropriateness and about people judging her or being embarrassed by it. I felt so unequipped to be A.'s mom.

In the meantime, A. seemed to be more disconnected than usual. Perhaps she sensed what was going on. She was biting her hand more and gritting her teeth. Scarier still was her propensity to shut down and be in her own world. Every sign of dysregulation fueled my anxiety.

I remember dropping A. off at her occupational therapist's office one day during this time. I was desperate to just
sit in a peaceful waiting room for 50 minutes while A. had her
session. When a very loud mom walked into the office with an
even louder young daughter who was constantly snapping her
gum, I wanted to scream. Didn't they know these 50 minutes
were my only quiet time of the day?

I didn't know what to do. It was hard to let go of my
dream that A. might still belong at Culver Academy. At the
same time, I didn't want to have to constantly *prove* to the
staff and teachers that she belonged there. I wanted her to be
embraced. At the back of my head, questions I wasn't ready to
answer yet were nagging me: did we want A. to fit in because
that was what was best for her? Or was that what was best for
me and Brian? Were we just catering to our egos?

After that conference, my anxiety shot through the roof
and I began thinking about A. every minute of the day she
was in school. What was she doing in the classroom? Was she
walking out of the bathroom with her pants down again? Was
she biting her hand, tuning out, sitting still in circle time,
interacting with other kids? Or was she comfortable in her
own little world, oblivious to the demands around her?

Winter break came and A. was so much calmer over
the few weeks that school wasn't in session. At our next
parent-teacher conference in early February, Ms. Rappaport
exclaimed, "Wow, A. has really turned a corner!" She told us
that A. was fitting in with the group and attending to tasks
alongside her peers. I exhaled. Everything was fine, I told
myself. I didn't need to worry.

But of course I kept worrying. At a classmate's birthday
party, I learned about Melissa, a mom with two children who
had originally both gone to Culver Academy. Her younger
child still attended, but they had placed her older child in an

intense therapeutic school called Cheerful Helpers Child & Family Study Center. Apparently after spending his formative years there he was now flourishing. Soon after, I ran into Melissa as we were picking up our children from school.

"Excuse me, are you Melissa Fullmore?" I asked.

"Yes," she said, her eyes warm and open. "Are you Susanna?"

I realized that one of the moms must have told her about me and I burst into tears as she squeezed my hands.

"I know," she nodded assuringly, and I had a feeling that she really did.

A few months later, I was driving to meet some friends for a coveted moms' night out when I received a call from Culver Academy. It was Friday night. Why was the school calling me? Maybe it was just going to be a recorded message, I thought, though deep down I knew it was something else.

"Susanna? Hi, Howard Carlton here. I just wanted to let you know that enrollment packages for the fall were sent home with the children today, but A. didn't receive one. We really want to see how things progress through the end of the school year before we extend an invitation for her to come back for her kindergarten year."

I remember pulling my car over to digest the news. I was all dolled up for my night out, but soon mascara was streaming down my face. "What do you mean?" I asked Mr. Carlton. "I thought A. was doing well?"

"We're just not so sure about her," he continued. "We'll let you know if we can offer her a space in the fall."

I hung up the phone without listening to any more of the nonsense and wiped away my tears, furious. Of course he was waiting to see who would commit to Culver Academy first before deciding if there was an extra spot for A.

I knew it was time to let go. A few days later, I finally

picked up the phone, called Culver Academy, and officially withdrew A. from the school.

Before I knew it, A.'s last day at Culver Academy had arrived. As I pulled up to the school for the last time, I thought back to 12 months earlier, when A. had received her acceptance letter. I'd been so elated that she was accepted into a typical private school. I was convinced that it marked A.'s graduation from the special-needs world. Sure, the therapies and doctor's appointments and assessments were cumbersome and expensive, but they had paid off! A. wouldn't need them anymore. I could sweep the special-needs chapter of our life under the rug and move confidently through life once again, knowing that I had helped my child overcome a huge obstacle. "Onward ho!" I had exhaled with relief.

I sat in my car for a minute with my stomach in knots, listening to the sound of birds chirping softly in the distance. My fantasy was finally at its end.

Still, no one would have guessed at how I was feeling as I walked down the long hallway toward Ms. Rappaport's pre-K classroom in my skinny jeans, flowy blouse, and freshly blown-out hair. If I couldn't control how my child would fit into a neurotypical school curriculum, I could certainly act like everything else in my life was ship shape. I grabbed the door handle and took a quick pause as I whipped my mouth into a forced smile.

There was A. gathered with all her classmates on the rug, waiting for me to join them. I sat down in the chair at the front of the room that Ms. Rappaport had set up for me and began to read A.'s favorite book to the class. Then A. gave out the goodie bags she had made for each of her classmates, excited to read their names and present them to each individual. I smiled through the lump in my throat as Ms. Rappaport snapped photos of our goodbye. "Please come visit anytime," she said to me as we gathered A.'s belongings.

A. and I said goodbye to the office staff as we left the building and walked out into the sunshine. A wave of hope swept over me. Maybe a new school would finally be the right fit for my amazing girl.

Truth Corner

Finding the best learning environment for your child

In the beginning, my ego as a parent completely got in the way of finding the best school for A. I tried so hard to have my child fit in even though I always knew, deep down, that she needed something else. I just refused to believe that the "something else" was a special education or therapeutic curriculum.

I also believed that A. needed to be around neurotypical kids. I didn't realize that she needed to be in tune with herself before she could tune in to others. It's such a spiritual lesson for all of us: we all need to get to know and understand our whole selves before we can embark on meaningful relationships with others. But when our babies are little, we have to steer that ship for them, and make sure we are providing them with the time and space they need to learn about themselves. We have to make sure that, whatever their schooling path is, they are being honored and encouraged to find out who they truly are.

Because I resisted the notion that A. might need something different than the plan I had for her, this resulted in her being in the wrong environment. In the special-needs world, early intervention is key, so losing that precious time is something I still kick myself about. I'm hoping you won't make the same mistakes I did, so I put together a few things to consider when you are trying to find the best learning environment for your child.

Be Honest

The best way we can support our child with different abilities is to be as honest and transparent as possible. Take a moment to really ask yourself: who is my child? What are their strengths? What are their challenges? What are my worries about my child? How is my child around other children? What is the picture I want to create of my child and how is it different than who they really are? What are my concerns and fears for my child? What brings my child joy? You can also ask the professionals who know your child like pediatricians, therapists, and teachers for keywords that would describe your child's strengths and challenges as well as for their recommendations on schools and programs.

Remove Your Ego

Let go of your own desires and ego and pay attention to what is the best environment for your child.

Don't Force It

Pay attention to moments where it feels like you are desperate or begging for your child to be admitted or accepted somewhere. Ask yourself why this feels so important. You want to find a place where your child feels welcome.

Do Your Research

Get to know the schools you're interested in. Take

tours, ask lots of questions, and talk to current families. Learn about the school structure, resource support, schedules, and class size. Sometimes it helps to visit the same school on multiple occasions to get a broader view.

Chapter 9

WHEN MELISSA FULLMORE first told me about her experiences with Cheerful Helpers, I was eager to learn more. The school's history was fascinating. It began with a group of women who banded together in 1958 to create a service agency and to support it with their own donations and fundraising. Initially, Cheerful Helpers Child & Family Study Center served young children with a variety of psychosomatic disorders. Soon they expanded their focus to all children with emotional and/or developmental issues and challenges. Cheerful Helpers became the first of its kind: a therapeutic preschool for atypical children.

When it became clear that Culver Academy was not the place for us, I knew it was time to reach out to Cheerful Helpers. After a conversation with Director Ellen Reinstein, I felt certain that this school should be our next step. But now weeks had passed since A.'s last day at Culver Academy, we still didn't have a start date for Cheerful Helpers, and I was restless and impatient. All the unknowns were giving me anxiety.

Soon I would learn that Cheerful Helpers moved at their own pace—they had a bigger therapeutic picture in mind.

Finally, Ellen Reinstein called to let me know they were ready to schedule our intake meetings, and that A.'s first day of school would be April 24th. I drew a big fat heart around the date on my calendar, and then I closed my eyes and prayed: *blessings upon blessings for this fresh start.*

When I first spoke with Ellen Reinstein, she had talked with me about teaching parents to fall in love with their children again, and this had stayed on my mind ever since. She explained that while parents experience an initial bonding with a newborn child, detachment can occur if the parent cannot form a relationship with the child, especially if a child is unable to connect.

I felt deeply attached to A. in so many ways. But I began to realize that our relationship was centered around my caring for her health needs: allergies, asthma, neurological discord. I was constantly in Go Mode—scheduling doctor's visits, driving to therapies, assessing her treatment plans. Of course I craved a deeper emotional connection with my child. But doctors had cautioned me that this would not be possible. The words of Dr. Lawrence at the Westside Regional Center echoed in my head: "Your child will never be able to have fulfilling, purposeful relationships with others."

I remember Brian and I drove together to our first intake meeting at Cheerful Helpers in silence. We'd been fighting more and more lately, and our last fight was still heavy in the air between us. I looked out the window feeling numb while trees, cars, and billboards whizzed by.

I was thinking about my mother. My father was very involved in our lives and engaged as a family man, but he also worked long hours and traveled. The day-to-day burdens of parenthood all fell upon my mother's shoulders. Whenever I asked her how she did it, she would simply answer, "I didn't know any different."

In a way, I realized, I hadn't known any different either. My parents' relationship had been my ideal. So when Brian went off to work every day, I automatically assumed I was responsible for everything else. I took on 100% of A.'s daily care. The stress of being home with a challenging child day in and day out wore me down. I felt isolated and lonely, as if Brian and I lived in different worlds, but then when we were together oftentimes we just got on each other's nerves.

I needed Brian's help but I felt like I couldn't ask for it because taking care of A. was supposed to be my job. I had wished to be a mother my whole life and now here I was! How dare I complain? I must admit, there was also a part of me that loved the martyrdom of having to do everything on my own. It was easier for me to focus on feeling like the victim than it was to take a hard look at how we were growing apart.

Brian and I had come out of our experience with Culver Academy in two very different places. When we'd first started to understand that something was different about A. and embarked on her therapy journey, I had felt such relief looking around those therapy waiting rooms at all the other parents, knowing we were all there for similar reasons. I felt an instant camaraderie with them because I didn't have to pretend my child was "fine" or try to cover up for her differences. As I learned more about the complexities of my child, I wanted to share the news with everyone I came across so that they could better understand our situation. But Brian felt more strongly than ever that we should not even discuss A.'s challenges with others because it might make them treat her differently.

Brian wanted A. to experience life as it was, without accommodations. On the other hand, what I had learned from Culver Academy—and what had brought me to Cheerful

Helpers—was that A. needed *more* accommodations, not fewer, so that she could flourish. It was getting harder and harder for me to stay quiet about A.'s needs, no matter what Brian believed. I felt like I was trapped in a bubble of inauthenticity.

Today's meeting was the beginning of Cheerful Helper's mandatory family counseling. After an intake session with Brian and me, we would soon begin play therapy sessions together with A. I was hopeful that this therapy could help us all. I was also afraid. What would happen if I really shared my deepest feelings and fears? What if Brian and I discovered that we weren't compatible after all?

When we pulled into the parking lot at the Immanuel Presbyterian Church where Cheerful Helpers was housed, I checked myself in the rear view mirror, making sure I looked presentable. As usual, I had hoped that if I seemed as pleasant and put together as possible, somehow I could smooth over all the discomfort.

Light beamed through high stained-glass windows in the church corridor as Brian and I headed toward the school office at the back of the building. I listened nervously to the echo of each step we took. At the door to the Cheerful Helpers office, I straightened my blouse and smoothed out my hair one last time, and then knocked gently.

Ellen Reinstein led us to one of the therapy rooms where we met our new family therapist, Mary Harris. Then Ellen and Mary began to ask us a series of thoughtful questions about A., our marriage, and ourselves. These were the kinds of questions we could only answer by tapping into our real feelings and digging deep. But I was so used to pretending that everything was okay that I didn't even realize how much I had been holding in.

When Ellen asked me about A.'s birth, I insisted everything

had been fine. As she continued with her questioning, though, suddenly I flashed back to that moment. I had been pushing and breathing and crying at the same time, exhausted in my active labor. A mirror was set up in front of my wide open legs so I would be motivated by my child's crowning to exert more effort into my birthing. That was when Dr. Hall decided to put a vacuum on my baby's head to get her out faster. I'd watched horrified as my ob/gyn yanked my daughter out and blood spurted everywhere, splattering his glasses.

"She just wanted to come at her own pace," I said and started to sob.

As I cried, I began to realize just how much I had been holding in all these years to keep moving and pushing forward. I had been a sensitive and emotional girl my entire life, but I had never experienced the kind of safety and openness to vulnerability I was feeling in that moment at Cheerful Helpers. I wasn't sure if I was ready for this. Transition and change had always been difficult for me. But either way, here I was—it was happening.

≪

"Mommy, I want to dress fancy for my new school," A. said the morning of her first day. She pointed to a bright turquoise dress in her closet with frilly edges.

"Can I wear that with tights, Mama? Don't you think that would be beautiful?"

"Sure, Peanut," I said. "You might be warm, though."

"No, it's perfect," she said. And it was. I could tell she was excited about the day, even though she would never admit to feeling that strong of an emotion about anything.

I brushed her hair slowly. I styled it a little extra special and topped it with a matching bow. Then I looked at myself in the mirror, staring at my reflection almost as if it belonged to someone else. What was I on this earth for? Was it just to be an advocate for A.? Was that enough?

A full school day at Cheerful Helpers went from 8:30 a.m. to 12:30 p.m., but that wouldn't be our schedule for a while. For the first week of school, A. would only be in the classroom for an hour and a half each day. There was an intentional, slow transition for new students.

For the first 12 weeks or so, I would also be in the classroom with her. This was meant to give both A. and me the time and space to be fully present in the process. Cheerful Helpers helped the child by treating the entire family, and my buy-in and involvement in the process would be paramount to A.'s growth and progress. I would be observing the teachers and therapists in the classroom and learning how to attach to my child in a new way.

The commute to Koreatown, where Cheerful Helpers was located, was a bit of a trek. It took around 45 minutes to get there, but I'd discovered a beautiful route through the historic Adams district. We drove past old Victorian mansions and lovely manicured lawns. Taking side streets was so much more interesting than sitting in bumper-to-bumper traffic on the highway. We passed new restaurants we couldn't wait to try: Korean BBQ houses, El Salvadoran pupuserías, sushi joints, taquerías, Papacristo's Greek Tavern. A. was perfectly content for the lengthy drive, looking out the window and commenting on all the new things she saw.

That first day we showed up at 9:15 a.m. on the dot. I remember nervously peeking through the window before the teachers let us know that they were ready for us to join.

A. and I were then introduced to our new routine. We would be welcomed into the classroom, school already in session, and A. would take her seat at a U-shaped table where teacher Rebeca sat at the head. There were four boys in the

classroom and one other girl. An assistant teacher named
Shetal and one or two other therapists were also in the classroom full time. That meant there was almost a 1:1 ratio of
staff to students.

I would take a seat behind A. and watch as Shetal would
assist my daughter closely. Every single second of the day was
a purposeful one. The kids were being taught how to be inde-
pendent, to learn about life, and most importantly, to express
their feelings. And the key to all of this was a constant commentary about their actions and behaviors; everything that
every child did was narrated by one of the teachers.

For example, if a kid was having a hard time, a teacher
would comment, "You're really having a hard time. It's hard
to sit in your chair and you are wanting to move your body."
Or, if A. dropped a pencil, instead of saying, "Pick up your
pencil," a teacher would narrate, "Oh, your pencil is on the
floor." The teachers constantly talked about what was happening, but they did not give specific direction for what the
child was supposed to do next. This way when the child would
eventually respond, it was as if the entire idea was birthed
from them. You could almost see the light bulbs flashing in
their heads as the children came up with responses based on
the outward narration of their actions.

This type of teaching was so different from anything A.
had experienced in her life, and it was just as new for me. I,
too, had been programmed to respond to requests, demands,
and questions. And I'd taught A. the same way I had learned.
Yet here was this seemingly simple and profound way for A.
to make decisions on her own, based solely on her awareness
of what she was or wasn't doing in that moment. This narration, rich with emotional undertones, was a new language for
both of us.

I thought back to our first therapeutic experience, years

ago, with a speech therapist. A. was not yet three years old. One of her biggest challenges was her lack of eye contact and connection with whoever she was supposed to be in communication with. The therapist would hold up treats like stickers and Skittles and have A. look at them for a certain period of time. Then she would reward her with the treats. It hadn't felt right. It appeared my child was being trained as a dog would be. But then I wasn't the expert. What did I know?

Cheerful Helpers was a whole new world. I watched as A. asked Rebeca, "Can I do a different puzzle?" A. was looking toward the trashcan on the other side of the classroom. Rebeca didn't respond until finally A. shifted her eyes. Then Rebeca nodded, as a visual response.

A. seemed to be interested in her teachers and classmates in a new way, too. She was making friends with Y., the other girl in the classroom. "I think you like cats, but dogs are my favorite," said my daughter, looking in the opposite direction of where Y. was sitting. Shetal narrated, "It seems like you're trying to say something to Y., but you're looking at the wall." A. shifted her body to face Y. and repeated the comment.

As a stay-at-home mom, I had spent so much time with A. But being in this classroom felt different. We were learning together.

In A.'s second week at Cheerful Helpers, things started to get harder. This was by design: now that the teachers had made a connection with my daughter and gained her trust, they were ready to help her bring some of her deeper, more difficult feelings to the surface so that they could be processed and healed.

One day, A. was writing her name at the top of her worksheet. Her letters were wobbly and she was pressing so hard with the pencil that the paper began to tear. "I am *not* a girl who likes to write!" A. blurted out, throwing her pencil to the floor and taking a big bite of her right hand. She turned toward Y., raised her hand and hit her arm. Shocked, Y. started to cry and called out, "A. hit me!"

Rebeca calmly narrated, "You are really frustrated, A. It was hard writing your name on the paper." She continued, "And take a look. Y. is crying. She's really upset." My stomach churned as I watched, wanting both to discipline my child and comfort Y. I felt completely out of control and like a failure for not raising my child right.

"I am mad!" Y. said, still whimpering. "Why did you hit me?"

A. bit deeper into her right hand as she stomped her foot into the ground.

Shetal jumped in, "You're hurting your body, A."

"I just didn't want to write my name!" said A. "I wanted to hurt Y. because I couldn't do my own idea!"

A. wasn't in trouble for her behavior. There weren't any stern words of discipline from anyone. I watched in amazement as the girls, prompted by the teachers, were able to talk about how each of them felt in that moment. The other kids in the classroom turned to watch the interaction. Each of them was soaking up the conversation. The girls were being given the emotional tools they needed to get through the moment. Soon after, they were working side by side again, peacefully.

Another challenge came when the Head of School, Ellen Pearlman, made her weekly visit to the class to do art with the kids. With red curls, a flowing caftan, and arms full of beaded bracelets, Ellen was both lovely and tough. That day, A. didn't feel like practicing doodling. "I don't like this plan!" she announced loudly before crumpling her paper and throwing it across the table.

Ellen spoke firmly. "A., We are doing art and our plan is to stick with art. Crumpling your paper just doesn't work."

A. started crying, tears streaming down her face. "I want to go home! I want my mommy."

As I watched my child come apart, I couldn't stop my own tears. But the teachers remained supportive and calm. They warned me that things would get harder for A. before she turned a corner. And for the next few weeks, the teachers were right. It did get harder. A.'s meltdowns in the classroom began to escalate.

As I watched my daughter struggle to find her words and voice, I struggled with my own emotions. I knew that Cheerful Helpers strongly believed that tantrums were important. Allowing A. to act out and have big feelings without trying to suppress them was meant to give her a chance to really feel what was happening within her in a safe and trusting environment. Narration could then provide language for what she was feeling and help her to understand and acknowledge what was happening in her body at that moment. Eventually, she would be able to use that language to express herself, and the teachers could then coach, guide, and encourage her to become more engaged with the world around her.

A.'s needs were becoming so much more apparent now that we were in this therapeutic environment. She had been able to pass as a somewhat typical child at Culver Academy because no one had been pushing her buttons or testing her limits. In some ways, this scared me and made me feel uncomfortable. The road ahead was a different one than I had imagined. Yet in other ways, it was a great relief. I noticed that I felt different now when I woke up in the morning. I was still exhausted from the emotional and physical demands of this schedule with A. But I had so much less stress in my life now that we were in the right environment.

Over the next few weeks, A. and I kept adding on to our time in the classroom until we were at a full, four-hour school day. Soon after this, we began to include short periods of separation into the schedule. For example, Shetal started taking A. to the restroom instead of me. Initially, when A. was having difficult episodes at school, I was instructed to hold her and wrap my arms around her body to help calm her. Now the teachers were taking over this role. "I'm going to give you a squeeze, A.," they would say.

I started noticing a weekly pattern for my child. Mondays were typically good days. A. seemed organized and regulated. As the week rounded out, however, she would get tired and run out of steam. She tended to be more distracted and tuned out. Then on the weekends she would recharge for the next week ahead.

One weekend in mid-May, A. was playing with a little girl at a family gathering. I couldn't believe what I was witnessing. She wasn't just playing side-by-side with her, they were actually interacting! Later, A. came to cuddle with me on the couch. She was connected, affectionate, and loving. When A. was first diagnosed with autism, I'd been told that none of this could ever be possible for her.

As A. responded more in the classroom, expectations from the teachers grew. She didn't like demands and kept pushing back. One day she was screaming so loudly that all of her classmates were covering their ears. Shetal noticed my discomfort and came over to me on the playground, out of earshot of any of the kids.

"You seem worried that A. is a distraction," she said.

I confessed that this was true and that it was difficult for me to watch her scream like that.

"It is so common to feel uncomfortable," she told me. "Remember, every child at Cheerful Helpers goes through this process. Some longer than others. And some louder than others!" I laughed and Shetal continued, "But it's important to trigger the biggest feelings we can. These outbursts are a positive thing. We are getting these children to really feel, sometimes for the first time in their lives."

The next weekend was my best friend Lola's birthday and we had planned a rare getaway together with our friends. Brian would take care of A. while I flew to the Bay Area for a girls' weekend. I didn't realize until I kissed A. goodbye and got on the plane how badly I'd needed to recharge my batteries. It was heavenly.

Back at school on Monday, though, A. was having her toughest day yet. She was extremely dysregulated, distracted, and tuned out. She was biting her hand constantly, nearly tearing her skin apart in the process. Soon she was screaming, too, and her teacher was holding her as I watched from a chair nearby. The teacher patiently narrated what A. was doing and how she was feeling. And then, slowly, A. started saying words. She was crying uncontrollably now, but snippets of sentences started to come out between sobs.

"My mommy left me!" she wailed, tears streaming down her cheeks. "I didn't want my mommy to leave me, but she did!" On a roll now, the words began to spill out. "I'm sad and I'm mad. Mommies aren't supposed to leave their children. And I didn't want to be with just my dad. I always need my mommy! I want my mommy and daddy to take care of me together."

I looked at my beautiful daughter who had never before expressed her emotional attachments to anyone in this way. Yet here she was, weeping and using words to share her feelings of abandonment. It was so hard for me to see my child's tears in this moment. I'd thought that she'd had a great weekend with her dad. If these were her feelings, I was afraid that I was oblivious to them most of the time.

Another day, A. hit Y. when they were learning to play tag

during outside time. The teachers and aides huddled around the two girls to talk it out. It took forever to process, and as I watched, I worried that A. would never be able to fit into a mainstream school ever again. Then I thought about J., a young man who helped out in the classroom a few times a week. He was in his early 20s and had just graduated from UC Berkeley. J. had attended Cheerful Helpers when he was a kid, too.

What were my goals and visions for my daughter? What was the measurement of success in this world? Did it mean just checking off a list of milestones: reading, writing, tying her shoes, opening a bank account, cooking for herself, driving? A friend whose child had been in therapies with A. since they were toddlers had once said to me, "Girl, all I need is for my son to graduate from college and get married and then I can go straight to my grave. My life will be complete!" We'd laughed then, but sometimes I wondered if all this worry and anxiety would ever really end.

Truth Corner

Co-parenting, communication, and community

I'd always thought that when I got married, I would stay married forever. My own parents met when they were young, and today they have been married for over 50 years. They are partners in life through ups and downs, joys and triumphs. But Brian and I were growing apart instead of being there for each other. And ultimately we decided to get a divorce. In this, we were far from alone. According to a recent study in the Journal of Family Psychology, parents of children with autism spectrum disorder divorce at a rate over 70% higher than those with neurotypical children. I would further venture to say that an even higher percentage would like to be divorced but can't due to the financial strain of maintaining two households. All I know is that marriage is full of challenges and that the stress of caring for a child with special needs tends to magnify all those challenges.

Since we had a child together but were going to live life separately, Brian and I had to make a conscious decision about how we would move forward. We tried to put our own issues aside to focus on A., but it wasn't always easy. Then again, none of this is easy! Whether you live with someone who helps you parent or not, whether you share parenting with a partner, with family, or with friends, here are a few things I've learned about co-parenting, communication, and community that might be useful.

Understand Yourself

This might seem like a given, but if we take a second to understand our intentions, our needs, and what we are hoping to accomplish, it will most likely be easier to have a parenting conversation, especially when a disagreement comes up. It helps me to focus on a simple mantra. For example, before I discuss anything with A.'s dad, I repeat to myself that my goal is to go with the flow and stay open to determining together what is best for A. I also remind myself that the strict way I was raised, even if it's what I know best, is not always the best plan.

Mindful Communication

Parenting with others is all about effective communication and that requires both conscious expression as well as conscious listening. There are also different types of conversations and they each come with their own challenges. Some are more spontaneous and in the moment, perhaps when a specific situation comes up in real time. Others are planned and may require a set time or space to talk through a specific topic.

It helps to figure out what communication methods work best for you and then to get clear on what your expectations of each other are. Do you communicate best via text? Email? Phone? In person? Do you have a set schedule for sitting down to talk, or do you just talk as needs arise? If one person has a topic they'd like to discuss, what is the time frame for that conversation? When should they expect a response? For example, when Brian and I need to discuss something in the moment, we pick up the phone, but we also always ask if the other person has the space and time to talk. If not, we set a time in the near future to have our discussion.

Remove Your Defenses

This has been one of my biggest learnings as a parent. We all have our defenses, but as someone who wants to control things, I probably have more than most. Sometimes I can be rigid and inflexible. But of course I can't communicate effectively with anyone if I have all my defenses up! That just shuts the whole conversation down. So before any conversation, I take a deep breath and challenge myself to let go of the reins and be open to the new. I can still be an amazing parent even if I am not always the one who comes up with all the amazing ideas.

Respect and Honor Each Other's Differences

We are all just doing the best we can with what we have. We all come from different backgrounds, upbringings, circumstances, and lived experiences. In moments of difficulty, a simple practice that can help is to imagine what life was like for the other person when they were a child. How were they raised? What were the circumstances around them? When we can respect where another person is coming from, it is easier to manage conflict and build trust together.

Ask for Third Party Help

I am a huge advocate for seeking out help when you hit a wall with your co-parent. Try reaching out to someone like a leader at your place of worship, a counselor, or a therapist who can help you move past that wall. If your co-parent isn't on board, make it clear that you want to keep the focus positive and on doing what's best for your child.

Build Your Community

How do we leverage our communities of family and friends in ways that are the most supportive not only to our children but also to ourselves? I have a big family and lots of close friends, and I have tried to bring them all into the loop by teaching them about what A. needs and how she best responds. I have taught them about her food allergies and how to avoid cross-contamination. All her cousins and my friends' children understand that they have to wash their hands after they touch dairy, eggs, nuts, or wheat. I have taught them about A.'s "truth serum"—her innate way of communicating her exact thoughts, without filter. I remind them not to take things personally. I also tell them that they can talk to her about anything and that if they don't like something, to speak up. When I see my friends and family supporting my child in these ways, I also feel supported. Their acceptance makes me feel held, nurtured, loved, and less isolated. A. has grown up with rich experiences at social events with family and friends, and I am eternally grateful to all the aunties and uncles and loved ones who have always had her back.

Chapter 10

IN THE FIRST phase of our experience at Cheerful Helpers, A. and I had learned to bond together, physically and emotionally. Now it was time to begin the second phase: Cheerful Helpers was going to help us practice separating in a way that allowed each of us to feel held.

As the week began, we pulled into the school parking lot and A. grabbed her backpack. Then she put it on her shoulders and started walking toward her classroom. This was the first time my daughter had put on her backpack unprompted. It felt like a victory.

Today I would be given 30 minutes away from the classroom, and I was determined to use my half hour well. I was feeling nervous about A.'s upcoming Individualized Education Plan (IEP), so first I jotted down some notes. I had a hard time listening to a room full of adults discussing developmental milestones that my child had yet to reach. I wanted to appear strong and capable—a completely functional advocate for my child—but sometimes I couldn't help but break down and cry instead.

As I wandered around the cafes and coffee shops of Koreatown, I wasn't sure what to do next. That morning, I'd weighed myself and found that I had gained some weight. I was feeling upset and annoyed about it, and also upset and annoyed that I was bothered by it in the first place. I felt out of control and I hated that feeling. I wanted to be able to fix everything, to tie it all up in a neat bow, but instead I couldn't seem to control anything at all—not even my own weight.

Soon my breaks from the classroom were increased to an hour and a half. It wasn't always easy to leave, either. Once A. was in the middle of escalating into an epic meltdown, and I wanted to stay and comfort her, but it was time for me to go. I tried to be productive, running errands, filling the car with gas, dropping off bills at the post office, picking up some things at the Filipino markets on Vermont Avenue. But I noticed that my life seemed to be either rushing around to take care of A. or these gaps in my schedule where I felt aimless and purposeless and as if I was just wasting time.

Toward the end of June, we had a one week break from school, and A. and I headed to Ohio to visit my parents. One of my sisters and her three kids would be visiting, too. I was looking forward to the usual swimming lessons, barbecue, and bike riding around Lake Antrim.

But this trip home felt different than usual. Or was it just that I was different? Though I'd had a few rebellious teen years, I had been a fairly complacent child. I hated conflict and always wanted everyone to get along. I didn't like to bring up things that were bothering me because I didn't want to experience the discomfort of talking through anything beyond the easy and uncomplicated surface of things.

Somehow, though, my months at Cheerful Helpers had begun to change this. When a conflict arose with my mother, instead of just letting it go like I usually would, I decided to speak up and share my feelings. To my surprise, she responded, "Well, if we are going to talk about our feelings, then here's how I really feel!" This led to a tough conversation, but the fact that we could be more honest with each other felt monumental. It turned out that Cheerful Helpers had been teaching me how to handle my big feelings, too.

As my breaks at Cheerful Helpers continued to get longer and longer, I began to get better at taking time for myself. I brought my journal with me everywhere, sitting down to write out my feelings. Sometimes there was even enough time to go to an exercise class. I noticed that I was also really missing my daughter and the other kids when I was gone. I wondered what was happening in the classroom that I had become a part of.

In mid-July, the moment finally came: I dropped A. off and left for the whole school day. For a little while, I lingered in the parking lot, peeking through the playground fence. I felt both a new kind of freedom and a lump in my throat. I realized that in our hours in the classroom, A. and I had built a new bond and had become closer than we'd ever been before.

A few months later, A. and I were at a play therapy session with our family therapists Mary and Dorrie. Brian was away for work, so it was just A. and me.

As I sat on the couch watching A. play, I was feeling giddy about the news from A.'s most recent neuro-psychological assessment. I couldn't wait to share it with Mary and Dorrie.

"The doctor told us that the sky was the limit for A.," I said, beaming.

At this, Dorrie looked at me gently and smiled, "Susanna, remember that the sky is the limit for you as well."

Her words hit me straight in the heart. I'd spent so much time all these years worrying about what might limit A. and trying to do everything I could to open up new possibilities for her. When was the last time I thought about my own hopes and dreams?

A. was sitting on a blue puzzle mat holding a plastic doll, playing a game she called, "What are my girl dolls feeling?" She often chose this doll at play therapy and would sometimes pretend that the crying baby needed to go to the doctor and get a shot.

Suddenly A. looked up from her doll and exclaimed, matter-of-fact, "Mommy, I just like the way I am!" Then she went right back to playing.

And finally, something clicked for me. The sky really was the limit for both of us as long as we could accept and love ourselves. I thought about all the years I'd spent trying to fix everything. Trying to fix A. Trying to fix myself. As I watched A. play with her doll, I realized that neither of us needed to be fixed. We were both whole and complete individuals, both on our own journeys in this life. We were both children of God. We both craved to be accepted, loved, honored, and heard for who we were. A. had just figured this all out before me. I realized that my child could be my greatest teacher, and that, at last, I was ready to learn.

I will never forget A.'s graduation from Cheerful Helpers. It was a hot late-July day more than two years after she started there. In the school's old church parlor a podium had been set up at the center of a small ring of chairs, and I took my seat alongside Brian and my parents, who had flown in from Ohio for the occasion. The room buzzed with the happy excitement of the graduating children's families.

Then the teachers led in their class. There were 12 students and three of them were graduating that day. A. wore a purple dress and her hair pulled to the side with a clip, looking very regal. It wasn't going to be easy for the kids to stay still during the ceremony, but the teachers were there to support them.

A. and two of her fellow graduates stood together and sang a song about a tree. They had known each other since they were two years old from various therapies, so this moment felt extra special. Then it was time for them to give their speeches.

When A. walked up to the podium, I felt a lump in my throat. It was hard to believe our journey at Cheerful Helpers was over. This was the speech she gave:

> When I was a new girl, it was hard for me to listen and I would throw pencils. I did not like to wait. I did not want to work and I would growl and howl and say, "I am going to eat you!" I would have a hard time with my teachers. I would say, "I just want to do my own idea." Shetal would say, "I am going to stop you, I know you are mad." I did not want to talk about my feelings. I would crumple up my paper and Rebeca would say, "That is not going to work." Now, I can do work and talk about feelings. Now, I can learn, I can do math and write sentences on my own. I learned that I can think. I found a rainbow ball and a biting ball. I am flexible when my friends have different ideas. Now that I am an elementary school girl, I can be flexible with my teachers.

I felt so proud, and I could see A. beaming with pride too. I couldn't help but shed a few more tears as my father congratulated her and called her his dumpling girl. Even though things were as difficult as they'd ever been between me and

Brian at that time, it felt good to be here all together, bursting with love for our little girl.

A. and I held hands as we walked to the parking lot after the ceremony, and I took a last look back at the school. Everything about this moment was different than what I had originally envisioned motherhood would be like. I had become part of a different community, a different kind of space, and I had learned a whole new way of understanding my child and my self.

The school's little yard was full of kids riding tricycles around a worn path, and I remembered that Cheerful Helpers promised every child would leave them with three things: knowing how to ride a bike, how to read, and how to make a friend. But A. and I were both leaving with so much more. We were carrying their teachings with us, and I felt again the sense that our possibilities were limitless.

"Should we say goodbye to Cheerful Helpers now, Mama?" A. asked me. She was peacefully munching on a vegan, gluten-free, nut-free cookie that I had brought to graduation for her.

I thought about a question that the Cheerful Helpers teachers would often ask: is it a big goodbye or a small goodbye? I asked A. what she thought.

"It's a small goodbye for now," she said, and I smiled, knowing she was right.

Truth Corner

The Letter A

I often think of how my journey with A. has been marked by the first letter of her name. First, A stood for her many severe allergies and learning how to keep her safe. Then A was for asthma as we discovered she needed breathing treatments. Next came Atypical Disorder as we began to be concerned about her non-neurotypical development. Soon that included uncovering another A—Auditory Processing Disorder. Finally, we received the formal diagnosis of Autism Spectrum Disorder as well as ADHD. And of course, throughout, there was always our dear friend, Anxiety.

It took me years to realize how A. was often defined by all these diagnoses, treatments, and interventions, by all these labels. They were what therapists and professionals used as guidelines to "fix" her. And somehow along the way, I had begun to allow these labels to define my child, too.

Finally I understood that A had to stand, first and foremost, for my child—my transparent, authentic, accepted, and loved child—not for any of the labels that preceded her. *This* was my real job. Sure, A. needed guidance and interventions to be at her best in navigating this life. But my work was to advocate for my child to be seen for who she is, in all her glory.

Affirmations

It was helpful for me to first understand and then know and feel in my heart that my child is absolutely perfect, whole, and complete, just as she is. I had to learn how to embrace that my child was a perfectly intact soul. And that this was just as true for me, with all of my own struggles and faults! One affirmation that I often repeat to myself during both the challenging days and the most beautiful and easy days is: "I am grateful for my child, coming to me as her mother, and embracing her for her absolute uniqueness. I love my perfect, whole, and complete child, brought to me by God. She is perfectly perfect. I am blessed that she chose me."

Acknowledgments

I am deeply indebted to so many people, and am grateful for the opportunity to thank them here (though I will certainly miss a few—I'm sorry!). First, of course, comes my family, who have each taught me a great deal in their own way. Mama & Papa Yang, Syd, Sarah, Sam, Shenandoah, David, Daniel, Melanie, Sofie, Adeline, Hudson, Christoph, Louisa, George-William, Pip, Teddy, Harry, Brielle, Anders: thank you for surrounding A. in love.

To my village: the huge number of "Aunties" and "Uncles" who make up a tribe of caring that have really come together to raise up this child of mine. Anita, Latarsha, Courtney, Gaia, Brianna, Poet, Yamani, Craig, Ruby, Dree, Bete, Sebastian, Derrial, KJ, Kay, Corey: thank you for making me feel less isolated every day.

To my SOUL SISTER, Lola Oladunjoye, who has seen it all from day one: thank you for the space to just be whoever and however I am in each moment.

To my Berkeley sisters, Natasha, Angela, Asha, Anita, Ruby & Melly: Go Bears!

To my girlfriends who GET ME! Thank you Shannon, Samantha, Rahsaana, Tika, Laury, Dawn, Barbara, Andi, Kristen, CK, AG (SiStars for life) and T-Bo.

To my fellow Autism Mamas, Rebecca Y, Kerrie G, Kim B, Barbara C, Kate H, and Carrie C!

Thank you to Ms. Gina (and the boys) for her next-level support as A.'s beloved behavior intervention specialist.

To the We Are Brave Together community (wearebravetogether.org) and especially its founder and director, my good friend Jessica (so grateful for you, JP)!

To my fellow soul care coaches and our fearless leader Suzi Lula: you are a touchstone I rely on.

To my Reiki Master Guru Beth, who helped my energy shift in a way both vital and seminal.

To Brooke Betts, who loved A. so much: LIVE YOUR LIFE.

To my superbly amazing hairdresser (and, therefore, therapist) David H, the very first person who A. trusted to cut and blow-dry her hair (a sensory milestone, indeed)!

To my biggest cheerleaders, Brian Altounian and Shawn Francis from the Just Two Dads podcast. You're the best.

To my Granderson Family, and the love they have given me and A. KJG: your inspiration and strength guides me daily.

To the Nelson, Lovell, and Lewis families, and A.'s dad, Brian.

To Cheerful Helpers Child & Family Study Center, especially my fellow Board of Directors members!

The phenomenal Kathryne Gogan at the Westside Regional Center has been A.'s case counselor since she was two and a half, and has been so helpful in getting us the resources and support we have needed. Thank you.

Karen Pittelman (my KP!!) at Writer's Remedy (writersremedy.com) has been essential in the writing of this book—we started this journey ten years ago and have gone so many places on this emotional roller coaster, and all the while you have been my therapist, my life coach, my cheerleader, my guide. You are the best. "We're getting sh*t done!"

For their help along the way, thank you to Social Foundations, Amanda OT, Sarah ST, Kristin ST, Dr. Anshu Batra, Robertson Pediatrics in Beverly Hills, F.A.C.T. Family, Ms. Valencia at Castle Heights Elementary, Ms. March at Palms Middle School, Dr. Knepper at Hami High, Ms. Latreasha, and Ms. Orley.

Nancy Broderick started as a fellow mom with an autistic child, and has been a beacon ever since. I love you, dear friend!

And my ancestors and loved ones who have passed away: Grandma Daisy, Ama and Agong, Grandma Sue, Grandpa Sedman, and my beloved San-Bei.

I think it is also important that we do something many parents of neurodiverse children find difficult: acknowledge ourselves and our hard work. So I want to do that here. I'm typically very hard on myself—always wanting to do better, to be better—but I want to acknowledge this part of me, the part who wanted to be a mother my whole life and had this vision of what it was going to look like: I would be a guide and mentor to a child who was super-well-rounded with good grades, who was polite and worldly and good at sports. And the other day I looked in the mirror and thought, "You are a phenomenal mother." I realized I have learned how to mother my child, this *particular* child, in the most authentic and life-giving and nurturing way. I cherish her. And as a result of being expansive in this way for my child I have learned how to mother myself, to take care of who I am intrinsically at my core. And I still wake up every day questioning myself, but I have no regrets about the way I have been a mother to A. And mothers: if we could just take a moment to affirm and acknowledge ourselves—all of us—we should be doing that.

And of course, finally, A. It's true what people say, that their child is their biggest teacher. But A. you have taught me in a way that I didn't know I needed to be taught. Children come through us, and I am so grateful you came through me. I remember when you were nine and we were giving a presentation together and a young person asked you if you'd rather you'd been born without autism. And you replied, so firmly, so confidently, "No. Then I wouldn't be who I am. I love myself exactly as I am."

Thank you.